*Engaging News Media*

COWLEY PUBLICATIONS is a ministry of the brothers of the Society of Saint John the Evangelist, a monastic order in the Episcopal Church. Our mission is to provide books and resources for those seeking spiritual and theological formation. COWLEY PUBLICATIONS is committed to developing a new generation of writers and teachers who will encourage people to think and pray in new ways about spirituality, reconciliation, and the future.

# Engaging News Media

## A Practical Guide for People of Faith

••• Mark Kelley

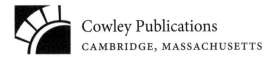

Cowley Publications
CAMBRIDGE, MASSACHUSETTS

Library of Congress Cataloging-in-Publication Data

Kelley, Mark, 1949–
    Engaging news media : a practical guide for people of faith / Mark Kelley.
        p.   cm.
Includes bibliographical references.
ISBN-10: 1-56101-276-9   ISBN-13: 978-1-56101-276-3  (pbk. : alk. paper)
1. Mass media—Religious aspects—Christianity. 2. Press. 3. Truth—Religious aspects—Christianity. 4. Truthfulness and falsehood. I. Title.
BV652.95.K45 2006
261.5'2—dc22

                                                              2006010446

Cover design: Brad Norr Design
Interior design: Wendy Holdman

This book was printed in the United States of America on acid-free paper.

Cowley Publications
4 Brattle Street
Cambridge, Massachusetts 02138
800-225-1534 • www.cowley.org

*To Marty, my partner in life*

# Contents

# Engaging News Media

# Introduction

... ye shall know the truth, and the truth shall
make you free.

• John 8:32

During times of universal deceit, telling the truth
becomes a revolutionary act.

• George Orwell

Absolute truth is a very rare and dangerous com-
modity in the context of professional journalism.

• Hunter S. Thompson

## Getting to The Truth

On the eve of the 2004 Presidential election, the air acrid with
assertions and accusations from both camps, a close friend of
mine, a man of immense integrity dedicated to peace, justice,
and the American way, plaintively ended our final pre-vote
conversation about which candidate was really best suited to
lead our country with these words, "Well, hell, Mark, how do you
know what *the Truth* is?" In just eight words (the length of a
perfect TV news sentence), my friend captured exactly what
this book is about.

It is hard to know what's true, and in these pages I will try to
shed some light on why. I will also offer some suggestions for
what we can do as individuals to come at least a little closer to it.
With humankind threatened by violence and greed perpetrated

by those who control the levers of power across the globe, the more truth we can discern the better: better for each of us, better for our sisters and brothers everywhere, and better for this shrinking, sometimes stinking, planet on which we all live.

> With humankind threatened by violence and greed perpetrated by those who control the levers of power across the globe, the more truth we can discern the better.

This quest found me at exactly the same time I started looking for it. It happened after I traded in the earpiece and stylish wardrobe they gave me to anchor the evening news for a bigger office and a lecture hall filled with first-year university students, a sizeable percentage of whom vowed to resist my every effort to get them to think about anything, let alone the Truth.

In fact, I had pulled onto this highway many years ago (imagine you hear the opening sounds from an episode of *The Twilight Zone*, and picture that wavy video thing they do on TV when they head into a flashback . . . ).

It was a dark, but not particularly stormy, morning on U.S. Route 322 between Hummelstown and Harrisburg, Pennsylvania. If my MG had sported a clock, it would have read approximately 4:30 A.M. I was on my way to WHP Radio, where I had recently landed my first job in broadcast news. I told friends and relatives I intended to be a Truth-teller. My religious commitment and values dictated that I make nothing less than a full-out effort to deliver important, useful, and accurate information to the radio audience.

On this particular morning, as on most mornings, I was already a bit apprehensive about how much news I would have to report when I sat down in the studio for my 5:30 A.M. newscast. At this point in the trip, I entered a web of criss-crossing interstates known as the Eisenhower Interchange. The Eisenhower had a reputation for nasty, often fatal accidents—bad news for the motorists involved, but fairly useful to the rookie newscaster looking for hard news to fill the first five minutes of his broadcast day.

I grappled briefly with the rather uncomfortable thought that I hoped to benefit from others' misfortunes on the highway, but quickly moved on to wondering if the local paper had covered whatever crack-ups the overnight hours delivered, and if the morning paper would be by the elevator when I got to the station. Assuming it was, and the police report appeared there, I quickly rewrote the details in broadcast form and headed for the microphone. Only later, as my journalistic skills grew and my work pace increased, did I have time to retrace the print reporters' steps and gather the information on the accidents from the police for myself.

It was then that I discovered that even the seasoned veterans of the Harrisburg morning paper could make mistakes; sometimes they completely omitted details of the accidents, and other times they reported other "facts" inaccurately. I had come face-to-face with a bedrock fact of journalistic life: discovering the truth and communicating that truth to a mass audience via print or broadcast is a daunting task, complicated by all sorts of factors.

It never crossed my mind in those days what an immense responsibility reporting the news is. I now realize the news can have a tremendous, sometimes destructive impact on people, those we report on and those who read, watch, and listen to our stories. A 2004 car crash in Maine illustrates the point. According to the original Associated Press account, seven people, three women and four children, died when their rented SUV swerved out of control and slammed into trees along Interstate 95 near Bangor. Only someone with a heart of stone could read those facts and not be moved by the magnitude of the loss. But the story went on to say that police estimated the SUV's speed, when it flew off the highway, at more than 90 miles per hour and only two of the passengers were buckled in. People wanted to blame the vehicle, one of those Ford Explorers that had been the target of allegations that potential mechanical failures left them unstable and unsafe. But police quickly ruled that out. Follow-up stories introduced other explanations for the tragically excessive speed: the women were racing to Northern Maine to see a man one of them met on the Internet or they were roaring up I-95 in search of medical care for a child suffering an asthma attack. If you bought the first explanation, any sympathy you had for the women would evaporate. If the second explanation were true, you might still question the driver's judgment, doing 90 mph on a busy Interstate with seven people in the car, but your condemnation might not be as severe. If the SUV's ill-fated passengers were part of your family, you now faced the dual challenge of finding the truth and dealing with your community's response to what people thought was true. In such cases, the reporter's accounts are all we have to react to. And we will react and form opinions and perhaps even act on those thoughts. The problem with this story, like many stories delivered to us by news media, is that the explanations we're reacting to are all hearsay. The reporter states them as fact but tells us nothing about how he knows if they're true, leaving us struggling to come to terms with another tragedy.

With all due respect to car crash victims whose stories I relied on to fill air time, no serious harm occurs when reporters mangle the basic, physical details of an accident, but the human details of a story like this one, and the details of many of the stories and events I covered over the years do matter. People of faith and good conscience need to be able to react to accurate, truthful reporting if they are to make critical decisions about their own behavior and the actions of those in their local community and elsewhere who control the levers of political and economic power in our society. This book seeks to explore journalism—the Truth-telling process—and the act of consuming journalism.

At the heart of everything that I will say in this book is the belief that we cannot take everything we see and hear and read in the news as gospel. Even if most journalists do a conscientious job of gathering information we need and want to know, for myriad reasons they still fall short of telling the whole Truth about our world. And that means we news consumers have work to do, too.

As sentient, intelligent human beings, we have a responsibility to think critically about the news that's delivered to us. If I made a mistake in reporting a fatal accident on the Eisenhower Interchange in Harrisburg, society wasn't likely to suffer any serious harm. But

> People of faith and good conscience need to be able to react to accurate, truthful reporting if they are to make critical decisions about their own behavior and the actions of those in their local community and elsewhere.

many of the issues and events reporters cover have far reaching implications that we need to understand clearly if we are to respond to them, as people of faith or simply as human beings who see ourselves linked to all of the other human beings with whom we share this planet. We need to pay attention to what's reported and notice what isn't. We need to know how journalists do their jobs and how we tend to respond to the information they give us. When we understand how the news works and how we work in processing the news, we can become active Truth-Seekers, taking charge of our communication environment and ferreting out Truth that will help us answer the age-old question: How then shall we live?

There's no getting around the fact that thinking critically about the news requires more effort than simply accepting on faith the version we get from mainstream media. But I believe the result is worth it. We will know the truth (or at least more of it than commercial news companies provide), and that knowledge—about our nation, our world, and ourselves—can make us better people.

# Chapter One

# What Is Truth?

Pilate said to him, "What is truth?"

• John 18:38 RSV

First thing out of bed in the morning, you grab the remote control on the nightstand and turn on the TV across the room. As you shuffle past it on your way to the shower, you glimpse images of a small, white house cordoned off on all sides by yellow crime scene tape. The street address flashed on the bottom of the screen indicates the home is in a pleasant, middle-class neighborhood a few blocks from where you're standing. The newscaster, a middle-aged woman you feel attached to after years of early morning electronic encounters, tells you, "Police found three bodies in the house, all of them shot in the head execution-style. Authorities also found a variety of drug paraphernalia. They say the shootings appear to be the result of a drug deal gone bad."

On your way out the front door, you find the morning paper jutting out of the shrub next to the sidewalk (the paperboy's aim has not improved). The top half of the front page is nearly covered by a color photograph of three bodies, the feet extending out from under green sheets, lying on the floor of what appears to be a ransacked living room. Above the picture, a banner headline reads: DOUBLE MURDER-SUICIDE CLAIMS THREE.

You toss the paper on the passenger seat in your car and flip on the radio as you pull out of the driveway. The ninety-second newsbrief on the oldies station where you catch *Imus in the Morning* has just started: "Police have not identified the victims, saying only that they are all members of the same family. Investigators suspect drugs played a role in the deaths."

Another day has begun, you're following your routine, which usually includes a couple of minutes under a hot spray in the shower, followed by periodic immersion throughout the day in a never-ending stream of information pumped out by newspapers, magazines, radio, television, and the Internet. You turn to the media seeking the truth, hoping to learn what's going on in your world. And, as happens many days, the precise shape of that information varies, at least a little, across the media that deliver it. The discrepancies may cause you to question the sources of the information, leaving you in a quandary: Who are you going to believe? Or will you believe any of them? How do you know, especially given their differences, which account is true? Why do you care if you're reading, hearing, or seeing the truth? What *is* Truth?

The simple act of posing the question begins to define the difference between the human animal and all other living species on earth. British philosopher John Locke, whose ideas undergird the American experiment in democracy, identifies Truth as a foundational element in human society: "To love truth for truth's sake is the principal part of human perfection in this world, and the seed-plot of all other virtues." Thomas Jefferson, who drew on Locke's thinking to compose the Declaration of Independence, concludes that "truth is certainly a branch of morality and a very important one to society."

But writers and philosophers warn that understanding the Truth is filled with difficulty. Only the ignorant or the foolhardy would attempt to answer the question—what is Truth?—with anything but humility. Novelist Oscar Wilde observes, "the pure and simple truth is rarely pure and never simple." Boris Pasternak wrote: "What is laid down, ordered, factual is never enough to embrace the whole truth: life always spills over the

rim of every cup." Roman procurator Pontius Pilate acknowl-
edged a struggle not so far removed from our challenge in the
face of each day's fresh batch of news, when he asked, with Jesus
standing by his side, "What is truth?"

Christians might find it a bit ironic that Pilate poses the age-
old question with the person they consider to be the ultimate
source of Truth an arm's length away. According to biblical accounts, Jesus parried both Jewish and Roman efforts to trap
him in a claim to earthly, political power, but he was absolutely
straightforward about his relationship to Truth. When Pilate
pressed him on his alleged claims to kingship, he defined his
life's work this way: "For this I was born, and for this I have come
into the world, to bear witness to the truth" (John 18:37 RSV).

> Jesus parried both Jewish and Roman efforts to
> trap him in a claim to earthly, political power,
> but he was absolutely straightforward about his
> relationship to Truth.

Of course, Christianity emerged from Judaism, and truth
lies at the heart of that ancient religion, as well. Israel's prophets
saw God and Truth as one and the same, and they believed that
the truthfulness of God obligated humanity to practice truthfulness in every aspect of their lives. The psalmist acknowledges
God as the source of all that humans should understand: "The
sum of thy word is truth" (Psalm 119:160 RSV).

Other world religions share the Judeo-Christian focus on
truth. Hinduism, which some of its adherents consider to be
the original religion and eternal law governing humanity and
the universe, is based on Sathya, what believers understand as
eternal Truth. In language not so different from Judaism and
Christianity, Hinduism teaches that Truth is the basis of knowledge, and knowledge can liberate us from a world of ignorance,
and set us free.

Buddhism, a self-described pragmatic religion intent on seeing things as they are, encourages its practitioners to embrace Four Noble Truths preached by the Buddha himself after his enlightenment. Those Truths are: (1) life is frustrating and painful; (2) our struggle to survive is the cause of our suffering; (3) we can end our suffering by developing a simple, direct relationship to the world; and (4) the path to liberation—*nirvana*—is meditation.

Finding the concept of Truth embedded deep in each of these world religions, religions born in cultures that span the globe, invites us to explore the universality of the need or drive to know, to understand, to grasp the meaning of human existence. Asking such questions, as suggested earlier, defines us as unique among the animals. But it does much more than that. Asking *why* we ask such questions connects us across the miles and the millennia to our earliest human ancestors. You may not have sensed the need to establish such a bond prior to this moment, but I believe a little time with our prehistoric ancestors will enhance our ability to define Truth and, in the end, improve our ability to recognize Truth when we see and hear it today.

Modern science traces our ancestry back as far as four- or five-million years, a length of time nearly impossible to contemplate. But those early relatives didn't ask questions, relying instead on instinct, much like any other animal, to survive in a potentially hostile environment. As millions of years rolled by, critical and wonderful and gradual changes took place inside our distant cousins' heads. Their primitive brains developed, according to some theories, what we know today as our minds. Professor of neurology Antonio Damasio argues that the brain, and its ability to pay attention, process information, think, and remember, improved our ancient relatives' ability to meet both physical and social needs, to survive. At this point, perhaps some 100,000 years ago, the questions started popping up, none of them foolish. What these early humans needed, urgently, was to know how it all worked. They needed to know why it grew light part of the time and very dark (imagine a world without electricity) other times, why they were warm sometimes and cold other times, how to find food, and how to avoid becoming dinner for creatures that shared their world. What they needed was the Truth. Paying attention to the world around them, seeing, hearing, feeling, smelling, tasting, trying to understand, to find meaning, became as much a part of their natural drives as the need for food, sex, or companionship.

They worked at preserving their existence without the benefit of the scientific method and the knowledge that illuminates our survival strategies today. As they stood on a riverbank in the morning and watched the fiery sun climb above the horizon, or sat outside their cave at night gazing up at the myriad pinpricks of light from the stars, they had no knowledge of chemical compounds, astronomy, or Big Bangs. But still they *thought*, seeking explanations for these elements and forces that influenced their lives.

From within this collective reflection, and with amazing consistency in cultures across the globe, came what we understand today as religion. For these early human beings, the unknown, mysterious forces—principally of nature—that seemed to control life and death must be the work of some supernatural power, and from that religious impulse came the urge to worship or appease the gods who held people's lives in their hands. In nearly every instance, shamans or priests rose up with responsibility for explaining the way the world works, and for teaching the people what the gods demanded in exchange for survival. There can be no doubt that the people, in their primitive circumstances, sought and welcomed such information. Again, in their need to know (inquiring minds have always wanted to know), they don't seem so far removed from those of us descended from them. And in both ages of humankind, we call the disseminated information, *Truth*.

The centrality of information seeking in the development of the human mind and human civilization connects us to current conversations in the world of archeology. I suspect many of us, in our study of social evolution, learned that early Homo sapiens were transients; we were taught that they spent their days in a hard-scrabble existence, wandering through the woods in loosely connected groups, hunting and gathering whatever they could find to fill their bellies. Then, about 14,000 years ago, when they learned how to stabilize their food supply by growing it themselves, they settled around the fields in cooperative farming communities and became people of the land rather than the forest.

More recent discoveries support an alternative sequence of events, driven, in the end, by the search for truth. Stanford University archeologist Ian Hodder contends that the desire to live together in community preceded the development of agriculture. Based on his work at Çatalhöyük, a Neolithic site in South-central Turkey (perhaps inhabited by our early relatives somewhere between 23,000 and 14,000 years ago), Hodder contends that the first people to call Çatalhöyük home chose it because it's near major clay deposits. Hodder and his colleagues have unearthed artifacts that indicate these prehistoric humans used the clay in their religious ceremonies. The land they would eventually farm is miles away from the tightly clustered dwellings which Hodder believes they lived in at the site. He and others suggest that the desire to participate in religious rituals and ceremony, not subsistence farming, may explain why traveling bands of hunter-gatherers chose to settle down. If they're right, those religious rituals and ceremonies most likely grew out of humanity's need to know the deepest reality of existence, the need for the Truth.

Religious rituals and ceremonies most likely grew out of humanity's need to know, the need for the Truth.

Throughout most of human history, religion and religious leaders—shamans, priests— have served as the principal source of Truth. For many people, they still do. But the spread of literacy and science, along with the advent of mass communication technology, has introduced a competing source of Truth—mass media. The power of mass media to spread information across the globe has overwhelmed the ability of religious institutions to control the Truth people are told. In our scientific, technological age, we can pick and choose our source of Truth. But as human beings, even modern ones, we still want to know, we seek to understand the world and our place in it.

Mass communications scholar Pamela J. Shoemaker makes the scientific argument for the connection between news media and our natural drive to know the truth. From within each of us, she believes, rises the urge to engage in surveillance of our environment, an evolutionary adaptation bequeathed to us by ancestors who spotted the tiger crouching dangerously outside their cave and escaped to tell the story; those who paid no attention to the approaching tiger wound up joining it for dinner, and whatever genetic contributions they might have made were lost to posterity. Shoemaker identifies two categories of information we seek: things that are not typical of everyday life and information that impacts our ability to function as part of society. She believes all human beings, including news professionals and news consumers, are "hard-wired" for truth.

> The power of mass media to spread information across the globe has overwhelmed the ability of religious institutions to control the Truth people are told.

Journalists rely on, and in some cases, prey on these basic drives in selecting news we will consume. Our ancestors learned to pay attention to unusual and unexpected events, like crouching tigers, to survive. News companies have long since discovered that they can tap into our instincts and draw us into their audience with stories about crime, or strange and bizarre human beings or events. William Randolph Hearst, one of the barons of the late nineteenth century era of Yellow Journalism (highly sensationalized and often blatantly false reporting) understood this principle very well, once observing that "the modern editor . . . does not care for facts. The editor wants novelty." We are naturally inclined to respond to such things even if they have little direct relevance for our lives. (Who hasn't slowed down to rubberneck while driving by a bad traffic accident?) Today's trend toward increasingly sensational news, even among mainstream news organizations, is evidence that this sort of journalism works, at least from the company's economic perspective. If audiences didn't assemble to take in this stuff, companies wouldn't bother to put it out. If we object to the trend, on grounds that it means less news coverage of critical social issues and events, the deepening immersion in infotainment might prompt both news companies and their audiences to respond that government and social problems have become routine and uninteresting, and their problems are unsolvable. And it isn't just an American phenomenon. Shoemaker confirmed her theory in a multi-national study, demonstrating that the desire for news about the world in which we find ourselves is virtually universal. With few exceptions, journalists in the countries Shoemaker studied chose to report information that fit into her two categories.

If we've followed the trail of civilization far enough to sense a common bond with our ancient human ancestors, and come to realize that our attraction to the truth rests on a natural drive far deeper than simple curiosity, we're making progress. We have touched on a number of dimensions of truth, but we have not yet managed to define it with any precision. In fact, we have tossed the term around a bit casually, at least as far as philosophers and theologians are concerned, even allowing for the possibility that the information delivered to us by twenty-first century news media might be equivalent to the Truth imparted by the overseers of Truth—priests and other religious leaders—in millennia past. Some observers have actually suggested that journalists, depending on how they do their job, constitute the prophets of our age, taking upon themselves the responsibility of announcing to all of us the Truth about our life and times. We'll consider that possibility in chapter three of this book. But before we attempt to measure and evaluate the nature and quality of the information media provide, we must attempt to define what we mean by truth, and related terms such as fact, knowledge, belief, attitude, and opinion. This effort is made in a spirit of humility (if Pontius Pilate and Oscar Wilde agree it's tough to pin down, who am I to try?), and in a spirit of simplicity, avoiding theoretical flights of fancy. That said, let's begin.

## Definitions of Truth

An Internet search for the meaning of "truth" yielded a daunting number of possibilities. Google turned up 48,600,000 websites that might contribute something to the cause of truth; 976,000 made some connection between truth and news media. Clearly, the reach of the electronic Web exceeds my grasp. The fallback option, dusty old hard copy dictionaries bearing fruits of hard labor accomplished by dusty old lexicographers of generations past, proved more manageable.

The word "truth" apparently evolved into contemporary English from an Old English or Anglo Saxon word spelled *treowth*, which meant faith or truth. I consulted several dictionaries for the meanings we now attach to the word, and discovered that the venerable *Oxford English Dictionary* provides a good summary of definitions that suit our purposes in this discussion. According to the OED, truth can mean: conformity with fact, agreement with reality, accuracy, correctness, verity (of statement or thought); something that is true, true statement or account, that which is in accordance with fact: chiefly in a phrase to say, speak, or tell the truth, to speak truly, to report the matter as it really is; true religious belief, often denoting a particular form of belief or teaching held by the speaker to be the truth; that which is true, real, or actual, reality, specifically in religious use, spiritual reality as the subject of revelation or object of faith; the fact or facts, the actual state of the case; and a verified fact—a point of true belief, a true doctrine, a reality.

Distilling all of these possibilities into a definition we can use in analyzing the truth content of today's "news" won't be easy. The breadth of meanings attached to this word reinforces Oscar Wilde's wit in observing, "the pure and simple truth is rarely pure and never simple." And to complicate matters further, before we can produce a standard definition of truth, we must spend a little time examining the words editors use to define it, words such as fact, knowledge, belief, justify or verify, and reality. If we gain some clarity on the meaning of these words, it should sharpen our focus on truth.

According to *Webster's New Twentieth Century Dictionary*, the word "fact" migrated into Modern English from the Latin *factum*, which meant that which is done, a deed, fact. A fact is something that has actually happened or is true, a thing that has been or is. A fact is also defined as reality, truth, actuality, the state of things as they are. If the truth equals a fact and a fact equals the truth, as the dictionary defines them, and we seek truth from news media, then news reports should be made of facts (like the example of the car involved in the crash in Maine, how fast it was going, or who was in it), and gathering in those facts should help us acquire a body of knowledge we can use to satisfy our basic drive for meaning and understanding.

But what is knowledge and what does it mean to know? The mere mention of the word knowledge sends the sprites and sylphs of philosophy flitting through the air in keen anticipation. Surely thinkers have spent as much time with these questions as they have with truth. The dictionary definition isn't tremendously helpful. Knowledge is: a clear and certain perception of something, the act, fact, or state of knowing; or information, the body of facts accumulated by humankind. "To know" is defined as: to perceive with certainty, to understand clearly, to be

sure of or well informed about (know the facts); or to be aware
of, to have perceived or learned. The word "perceive" threatens
to cloud the water a bit. It lacks the figurative firmness of "fact."
It's tempting to follow it down the rabbit hole right now, but we
won't. Instead, we turn to that ancient seeker of truth, Plato, for
help in defining knowledge. In his *Theaetetus*, the great thinker
contends that knowledge is justified true belief. It's reassuring
to see the word "true" in this definition, but "justified" and "belief" need some work

"Belief" can mean several things: an acceptance of something as true, faith, or a firm persuasion of the truths of religion; a creed or body of religious doctrine; and an opinion,
expectation, or judgment. The middle sense (a creed) doesn't
really apply to the information we get from news media (at least
I hope not), and the last sense (an opinion) seems even softer
than "perceive," which leaves us with belief as an acceptance of
something as true. If we plug that into the definition of knowledge, we get "justified true truth." The meaning of "justified"
becomes very important in this context. To justify something,
like a fact, is to demonstrate or prove that it is right or valid, to
verify it. (Reporters could tell us how fast the SUV in the crash
in Maine was going after police used their scientific investigative tools to examine the evidence at the scene.) "Verify" can be
defined as to prove the truth of something (like a fact reported
by news media) by presentation of evidence or testimony, to
substantiate. Knowledge, then, for our purposes, is an accumu-
lation of facts (presented by news media) that we believe to be
true because they have been justified, verified, or proved to be the
truth. At least that's what we might expect journalists to deliver.
(We'll examine the expectations and intentions of news producers and news consumers in chapter three of this book.)

And then there's "reality." Several of our definitions of
"truth" equated truth with facts and facts with reality, and implied that "reality" is *what is*. (When police reported that they
found the SUV in the fatal Maine crash lodged against trees

alongside the highway, they were making a statement of fact, a statement about the reality of the situation.) *The American Heritage Dictionary of the English Language* defines "reality" as: the quality or state of being actual or true; the totality of all things possessing actuality, existence, or essence; and that which exists objectively and in fact. We could, no doubt, discover more philosophical or theological assays into the meaning of reality. But, for the moment, these definitions of reality remind us that a definition of truth suitable for a discussion of news media must be founded on an objective, factual view—a realistic view—of the world we seek to understand.

We've tripped through our list of truth-related terms. Do the bits and pieces we've uncovered add up to a definition of truth that will support us as we wade into the fast-flowing torrent of information dumped on us twenty-four hours a day? Our review of formal definitions revealed several faces of truth. We discover some truth by observing the world around us and testing the validity of our perceptions. We call this truth "facts" which, when connected together, grow into knowledge. We know these facts are true because they have been verified and proven. Other truth we accept as true because we believe it to be so. Often these understandings are communicated to us by religious leaders, as the ancient shamans shared the truth with our early ancestors. This is the Truth of religious faith. The definitions identify a third type of Truth, divinely revealed Truth. For people of faith, this is truth with a capital "T." The *Theological Dictionary of the New Testament* describes this type of truth as a religious reality accessed through religious feeling which allows human beings to know God—the Truth.

Which of these types of truth can we expect from professional journalists and news organizations today? All of them? None of them? As I mentioned earlier, some people see today's journalists as latter-day prophets, assuming the role of the priests in ancient times, disseminating Truth about the state of our societies and our world to the masses forgotten or abused by the great financial and political powers of our times. In Paddy Chayefsky's classic film *Network*, TV anchorman Howard Beal, possessed by a strange spirit of disclosure, brings viewers a harsh vision of our times, ultimately urging them to throw open their windows and shout, "I'm mad as hell and I'm not gonna take it anymore!" Beal's encounter with the corporate god who owns him and his network drives him to distraction and death. Chayefsky communicates a harsh truth about society and mass media through his "mad prophet of the airwaves."

Some people see today's journalists as latter-day prophets...disseminating Truth about the state of our societies and our world.

Other observers accept the terminology, but turn it against the news media, accusing them of functioning as false prophets, especially in their coverage of environmental issues such as global warming. These forces, generally of a conservative political persuasion, accuse reporters of embracing apocalyptic predictions of global disaster so thoroughly that they now function as the priests of the environmental movement, preaching (no longer simply reporting) false truth to the public. Critics from the left accuse news organizations of preaching the company or government line. In 2005, liberal critics tagged networks and national newspapers as false prophets in their pronouncements about America's successful war in Iraq.

An increasing number of people condemn the news media and their staffs for abandoning the truth-telling function entirely, offering in its stead a sensationalized, commercialized product more responsive to the economic tug of broadcast ratings, circulation numbers, and advertising revenues than to the people's natural need to know. For these citizens, the news is the last place to look or listen for information that quenches the desire for truth. Others hold a less caustic view, clinging to the hope that *some* commercial news media and a greater portion of public media will continue to tell the truth we must have to understand and survive in an increasingly multifaceted and interdependent world. Indeed, some still consider truth telling a critical responsibility for journalists. As citizens willing to accept responsibility for making decisions about government and communities and, ultimately, contributing to the well-being of society, the need for the truth remains at least as urgent as it was for our early human ancestors.

After laboring in the journalistic trenches for several decades it seems reasonable to me to expect journalists to tell the truth. The vast majority of my colleagues over the years claimed that they entered the news business to do that. Enthusiasm for getting the whole truth, the ugly truth, the vital truth may have been greatest in the early 1970s, when reporters helped expose a series of criminal acts and dirty tricks carried out against the Democratic Party and others by President Richard Nixon and his reelection team. (The revelations, known collectively as the Watergate Scandal, made Nixon the only President ever to resign and shattered the public's belief in government as a source of truth), but I believe the desire to tell the truth remains. Unfortunately, as we'll see in chapter three of this book, that desire often does not translate into delivery of the whole truth.

The big question is: Which type of truth do journalists want to tell? At the risk of disappointing some readers, and alienating others, I would argue that it is, for the most part, the objective, factual kind, the kind that can be tested, investigated, and verified. That doesn't mean journalists have no interest in religious truth or divine revelation. My understanding of religious truth serves as a primary foundation for my work as a professional journalist. The central tenet communicated to me by my faith is that each of us has a responsibility to care about those around us and seek justice in society. I have tried to address those obligations through my work as a journalist, in the stories I chose to cover and the truth I tried to tell about the issues and events involved. (We'll examine where most journalists stand on faith and values questions in chapter three.) But if we go to the news media looking for reportage that reflects a particular set of personal values and religious convictions— our values and convictions—we run the risk of being severely disappointed.

That being said, how well do journalists, especially the mainstream, commercial news media, do in reporting even factual, verified, objective truth? And what sort of threats, temptations, limitations, and constraints do they have to fight their way past to bring it

> The big question is: Which type of truth do journalists want to tell?

to us? In chapter three, we'll examine these questions from a number of directions. But before we look outside at news media and professional news workers, we need to look inside for a moment. The conclusions we reach about journalists and the news they report, our understanding and evaluation of the truthfulness of the information they deliver, are all subject to processes operating in the minds bequeathed to us by ancient Homo sapiens. To grasp who reporters are and what they're trying to say to us, we first need to be sure we know the "truth" about ourselves. That's what we'll consider in the next chapter.

# Chapter Two

# The Personal Challenge: Sensing the Truth

> The fault, dear Brutus, is not in our stars, but in ourselves.
>
> • *Julius Caesar,* Act I, Scene Two

## The War Inside Our Heads

October 30, 1938, in New York City, began in a fairly ordinary way. Skies were cloudy, the temperature a little colder than the day before. The *New York Times* informed readers that Poland and Germany were talking abut Germany's mass deportation of Polish Jews (10,000 had been sent "home"), Jersey City's mayor (fearing a "Red Riot") had refused to allow a rally where the ACLU's president was to speak, and the Fighting Irish of Notre Dame had rolled over Army's football team in Yankee Stadium on Saturday. All in all, not an unusual day. But by 9:00 P.M. (Eastern Time) that would change, leaving this day seared into the memory of millions of Americans. Most people later said they were completely surprised by what happened. Had they read all of the Sunday *New York Times,* however, they might have spared themselves some trauma by noting, in the radio listings for this night, that WABC planned to present a play from 8:00 P.M. to 9:00 P.M. The author: H. G. Wells. The title: *The War of the Worlds.*

The broadcast began, right on time, at eight o'clock. An announcer intoned: "The Columbia Broadcasting System and its affiliated stations present Orson Welles and the Mercury

Theatre on the Air in *War of the Worlds* by H. G. Wells." The
weekly show's familiar theme music flowed into American
homes as the announcer introduced Orson Welles, the director and star of the Mercury Theatre On The Air. Welles, a
bright young man destined to leave his mark in radio and film,
launched into the performance, an adaptation of H. G. Wells's
science fiction account of a Martian invasion of the earth. This
night, thanks to modifications by writer Howard Koch, the
Martian cylinders would land in New Jersey, and across the
country, in places listeners recognized. It was just a radio play,
put on by a company of actors and actresses who, after seventeen installments, were familiar to millions of people who rou-
tinely gathered around the radio seeking entertainment on a
Sunday night. Six- to twelve-million listeners may have tuned
in for what Welles told the audience, *at the end of the program,*
was "the Mercury Theatre's own radio version of dressing up
in a sheet and jumping out of a bush and saying Boo!" on the
night before Halloween. Welles's little
joke worked, too well. By nine o'clock
that night, millions of Americans, panicked by the program's detailed descrip-
tions of the Martian attack, had loaded
children, belongings, and family pets into
their cars and headed into the night to
escape the aliens.

> Millions of Americans, panicked by the program's detailed descriptions of the Martian attack, had loaded children, belongings, and family pets into their cars and headed into the night to escape the aliens.

The next day's *New York Times* up-
dated the struggles of deported Polish
Jews, but the biggest article, two columns
worth, elaborated on the headline: Radio
Listeners in Panic, Taking War Drama as
Fact; Many Flee Homes to Escape "Gas
Raid From Mars," Phone Calls Swamp
Police at Broadcast of Welles Fantasy. Vir-
tually anywhere the broadcast reached,
according to the *Times*, it "disrupted

households, interrupted religious services, created traffic jams and clogged communications systems . . . at least 20 adults needed treatment for shock and hysteria."

The newspaper offered a sampling of reaction, gleaned from across the country: A Bronx resident told police, "They're bombing New Jersey." In San Francisco, a distraught caller pleaded, "My God, where can I volunteer my services? We've got to stop this awful thing." Men and women wandered into neighborhood streets in St. Louis wondering how to deal with the "sudden war." A Baltimore woman booked a flight to New York City to rescue her daughter who was attending school there. Weeping, hysterical women called the Providence, Rhode Island newspaper asking for details, while a Boston woman told a newspaper she could see the fire from the attacks. Switchboards at police stations, newspapers, and radio stations were deluged with calls. One Virginian called to tell the local paper they were all praying. A woman ran into an Indianapolis church screaming, "New York has been destroyed." A Kansas City caller requested more information about meteors landing in Salt Lake City. And a Pittsburgh man reported coming home part way through the broadcast to find his wife ready to poison herself rather than die by alien monsters and their lethal gas. Her husband talked her out of it.

Public reaction to *War of the Worlds* raised lots of questions, including questions about news judgment and treatment by media organizations. At least one Congressman called for hearings into a medium capable of frightening millions of Americans out of their wits and endangering the public. But the most profound investigations triggered by the radio show had to do with how we, as human beings, work; specifically, how our minds work in processing any information that we take in through our senses. Not everyone who heard part or all of the broadcast panicked. Why not? Observers started speculating about that as soon as the program signed off.

The quick response, documented by reporters the next day, proposed that those frightened by the radio play either missed

> The most profound investigations triggered by the
> radio show had to do with...how our minds work in
> processing any information that we take in through
> our senses.

or did not listen to the opening of the show, which clearly identified it as a radio play. Panic may have ensued more readily
if readers failed to notice the listing for the program in the
*Times*'s weekly radio guide. Going off the deep end also meant
missing three more announcements *during the broadcast*,
which stressed that the show was fictional. The network knew
full well the extent of reaction to the program before it ended
and took steps to reduce the nation's anxiety level. After the
broadcast, at 10:30 P.M., 11:30 P.M., and midnight, announcers
reminded listeners that Welles's broadcast was an adaptation
and the entire story was fictitious. In addition, an estimated
60 percent of local stations provided their own on-air re-
assurances that listeners had nothing to fear. Americans who
headed for the hills somehow managed to miss most of the
post-broadcast disclaimers, too.

The longer, more scientific explanation for how that could
happen came through the work of a psychologist named
Hadley Cantril. Cantril was an associate director, along with
Frank Stanton (later head of research for CBS) of the Office
of Radio Research at Princeton University. The Rockefeller
Foundation funded the center and assigned it to study the role
of radio in the lives of listeners in the United States. When the
Radio Research project opened its doors in the fall of 1937,
there were about thirty-two million families in America and an
estimated 27.5 million of them owned a radio. One year later,
the *War of the Worlds* broadcast provided a tremendous op-
portunity to examine how radio, by far the dominant mass medium in America by this time, impacted the lives of the people
it reached. Cantril's work also shed light on the inner workings

of our minds, and contributed to efforts to understand what happens when the world around us and the world within us collide.

Cantril and his colleagues studied social psychology; they sought to understand how human beings interact with the world around them and form attitudes and beliefs that guide their behavior. They chose a very difficult subject, and one that has aroused considerable controversy over the years. The biggest obstacle psychologists face is that, unlike natural scientists, they can't dissect thoughts and opinions or run them through a centrifuge to distill their essential ingredients. Today, scientists have developed machines that can detect activity in specific parts of the brain; scanning machines produce electronic images that change color in areas where we think certain types of mental activity are going on. Researchers are trying to pinpoint the exact, physical location of a specific bit of knowledge, the concrete presence of an attitude or belief. But in the 1930s, psychology was at a far more basic level. As they struggled to understand how we think and feel and act, how our minds actually work, these scholars had to work outside our heads. The only tools they had were observation of our behavior and examination of our spoken words. They searched those for patterns and tendencies that might explain how our minds operate and why we think and act the way we do. From their findings they constructed theories, which psychologists have been testing, amending and expanding ever since.

These research methods may strike us as a bit less precise than the tools used by natural scientists; we may want to *know* exactly how the mind works. But these are the methods they use. It is important to be aware of that as we examine their analysis of the panic that gripped many Americans (and Canadians) during the Mercury Theatre's broadcast of *War of the Worlds*.

We should also bear in mind the cultural climate into which Welles and company beamed their Halloween prank. Until the mid-1800s, mass communicators reached people in the United

States through magazines, books, and newspapers. Then Samuel F. B. Morse harnessed electricity to produce the telegraph. Appropriately, the first official words he transmitted were: "What hath God wrought?" The message captured the awe with which Americans greeted this new invention—a machine that could rocket human communication from one place to another with lightning speed. In an instant, the telegraph shattered people's horse-drawn concepts of space and time. Crowds gathered around local telegraph offices to marvel at what this instrument could do, even if they didn't understand enough about electricity to know how it did it. The great minds of the nation predicted that dissemination of important ideas and knowledge through this medium of mass communication would raise the intellectual and cultural level of our people and radically improve our communication with other nations. Some observers considered the telegraph a giant leap toward world peace.

As innovators found new applications for the technology, however, some unanticipated side effects developed. Specially adapted telegraph machines put business managers in touch with their operations and activity on Wall Street as never before. Suddenly, a plant manager who normally had days or weeks to think about ordering materials or shipping orders was expected to react to information immediately and make snap decisions. A query that arrived by telegram carried with it pressure to compose a prompt reply (not so different from the expectation that accompanies many of the email messages that assault our computers each day). This revolution in communication proved too much for some businessmen. They succumbed to an alarming case of bad nerves. Ordinary working folks, not exposed to this relative flood of information, likely avoided the condition, but across the nation thoughtful people in all walks of life may have begun to wonder just what the telegraph had wrought in our society.

The twentieth century arrived with another dazzling form of mass communication—moving pictures. Capitalizing on basic principles of human information processing, filmmaking quickly grew into a lucrative industry, attracting millions of viewers, who flocked to theaters, in the beginning, to see projected images of horses running on a track or a locomotive pulling into a railway station. The techniques and the subject matter quickly became more complex and sophisticated. By the 1920s, an ample dose of sex and violence awaited young and old alike at the local cinema.

The content generated concern for parents and attracted the attention of politicians. Both groups feared that exposure to such realistic portrayals of questionable behavior might corrupt America's youth and ultimately unravel the moral fabric of society. Embedded in their thinking was the suspicion, sometimes summarized as the Magic Bullet Theory, that simple exposure to a movie could fire ideologies, values, and behaviors into our children, with significant influence. Underlying the theory was a belief that common people, especially, did not possess the mental ability to process this information, leaving them highly vulnerable to harmful messages.

In the late 1920s, a social scientist named Herbert Blumer hired on to investigate the impact of films on youth. After interviewing dozens of children and adults, Blumer published a report that seemed to confirm people's fears. He concluded that people watching movies, adults and children, experience "emotional possession." They surrender their minds so thoroughly to what they see and hear that the picture takes control of their emotions, arousing (in children) terror and fright, excitement and passions of love in teenagers, and sorrow and pathos in most people. Based on his interviews, Blumer credited films with stimulating people to imitate cinematic behaviors related to their appearance, mannerisms, courtship practices, even how they made love. He concluded his statement by speculating on how broad the influence of movies might be. Films, he wrote, "may furnish people with ideas as to how they should act, notions of their rights and privileges, and conceptions of what they would like to enjoy. We have indicated, finally, how motion pictures may implant attitudes." The public accepted Blumer's work as truth they should be very concerned about. Families and politicians pressured filmmakers to modify their product to reduce its threat, especially to their children. Because they wanted to keep the seats filled in the theaters and avoid government control of their industry, Hollywood censored itself, ushering in an era of sanitized storylines and more wholesome portrayals that would extend into the early days of television.

Over the same decade, with the public's fondness for film tempered by concerns about the impact mass media might have on their children and themselves, radio took to the airwaves. It was love at first listen. People read the paper less and tuned into radio more and more. They depended on radio to connect them with the rest of the country and the larger world. They trusted radio to bring them information and knowledge. They believed what radio told them. As with the telegraph, some admirers predicted that this latest innovation in mass communication would usher in a new age of enlightenment, raising the level of cultural appreciation in the United States and carrying us to a new level of peace and security around the world. Then, on October 30, 1938, a Sunday night, Orson Welles and the Martian military fleet attacked the United States and all hell broke loose.

It was this American society, still telling each other stories of that scary night, that Hadley Cantril and his colleagues proposed to examine in an effort to explain why so many people panicked during a radio play. By now, this society had racked up thousands of hours of mass media exposure. But in the years since Morse catapulted human communication and human sensibilities over the barriers of space and time, this society had endured events that inflicted pain and suffering,

> They trusted radio to bring them information and knowledge. They believed what radio told them.

not awe and inspiration. Civil war had claimed the lives of thousands of America's sons and threatened to dissolve the Union. A megalomaniacal newspaper publisher deceived his readers and shamed the President into duking it out with Spain over what was most likely a munitions accident aboard an American warship in Havana Harbor. A World War early in the new century left thousands of American soldiers dazed and maimed and dead. Impulsive and greedy speculation brought down the stock market and plunged the nation's economy into a ten-year long slough of depression that reduced millions of Americans to relentless poverty and hunger. And with their heads barely above water, citizens could hear the drumbeat of another military cataclysm approaching.

Trying times to be sure, but does the turbulent social and political history of the United States during the decades leading up to October 30, 1938 explain why millions of Americans would panic during a radio play that amounted to nothing more than a clever adaptation of a science fiction novel written forty years before? As skilled psychological researchers, Hadley Cantril and his colleagues took these events into account, but they would serve as only part of the group's final report.

Others had begun searching for answers almost as soon as the broadcast was over. Surveys commissioned by the Columbia Broadcasting System and the American Institute of Public Opinion reached conclusions similar to the speculation offered the next day by journalists—listeners who mistook the play for an actual news report (the truth) probably tuned in late and missed the disclaimers at the beginning of the broadcast. Cantril and company noted these findings in their account of what happened, but they attempted to delve deeper into the psyches of those who experienced the broadcast. They conducted extensive interviews with 135 people, all in the New Jersey area, chosen through a method know as "snowball sampling," in which an interview subject recommends others who might be useful to the interviewer in exploring the subject of interest. A snowball sample is not the most scientific method available to social scientists. The results may not be as reliable as those from a randomly chosen group. Random selection increases the likelihood that the conclusions reached with one group of subjects will be fairly close to those of any other randomly chosen group.

Cantril and his colleagues confess the limitations of their study (limitations imposed largely by funding constraints) in a book published by Princeton University Press in 1940 entitled *The Invasion From Mars: A Study in the Psychology of Panic*. On the title page, Cantril recognizes the assistance of two other researchers: Hazel Gaudet and Herta Herzog. Gaudet would later contribute to an important communication theory known as the two-step flow, which argues that information from mass media is more likely to flow first to opinion leaders, who process it and then pass along what they consider important to opinion followers, who depend on opinion leaders' judgment in forming their own attitudes and opinions. Herzog continued with audience research after the *War of the Worlds* broadcast, producing important insights into why daytime radio listeners sought out particular programs. If they tackled the same project today they might try to explain why some radio listeners tune in to Rush Limbaugh and others find National Public Radio closer to their gospel truth.

Cantril, Gaudet, and Herzog belonged to a phalanx of bright, young, social psychologists drawn to the study of mass media by allegations, expressed most sensationally in the Magic Bullet Theory, that media messages, films and radio shows, had a powerful impact on human beings. For these social scientists, the timing of *War of the Worlds* couldn't have been better. Their findings, despite any scientific misgivings about their method, mark an important step forward in mass communications research and in our understanding of the way our minds deal with whatever the world sends our way.

Cantril and his small army of interviewers asked people a

host of questions in their search to understand why some people panicked during the broadcast and some did not. They wanted to know when, where, why, and with whom people tuned in that night. If subjects said they knew it was a play from the beginning, interviewers asked them how they knew, did they ever have second thoughts about that, and why did they think others became frightened and hysterical during the broadcast. Those who admitted thinking, at least in the beginning, that the broadcast was a real news report were asked how long they believed that and how they eventually discovered they'd been fooled. "Believers" also answered questions about whether some form of life exists on Mars, how they reacted to past crises such as war or natural disasters, whether God controls events on earth, and what fears or prejudices they harbored. The interviewers recorded basic demographic information on all of their subjects, including their age, occupation, education, religious involvement, political affiliation, and media use. Interviewers were encouraged to include their impressions of the person's personality and psychological state.

From all of the information they collected, Cantril's group identified several factors common to those who *did not* panic during the broadcast. These individuals, Cantril reported, were skeptical, unwilling to jump to conclusions, tended to examine evidence and verify information (such as content delivered via radio), had special knowledge or training related to the broadcast, and used that knowledge to decide what to make of the program. All of these people, according to Cantril, possessed a common, overarching quality that the researchers labeled "critical ability." Cantril defined critical ability as the "capacity to evaluate the stimulus [in this case, Welles's radio play] in such a way that they were able to understand its inherent characteristics so they could judge and act appropriately." A major element in critical ability, according to the study, was education. High school and college graduates were far less likely to fall for the hoax. Education remained an important part of the explanation, no matter how old the person was or how much money she made.

But the researchers reported that even the power of education could be overridden by several factors which might undermine critical ability and tempt the person to believe the broadcast was a real report of an unfolding catastrophe. These factors fall into three basic categories: personality characteristics, characteristics of the place where the person listened to the program, and unstable social conditions. Personality characteristics suggested by Cantril and company included: insecurity, phobias, how much an individual worried, lack of self-confidence, fatalism, religiosity, and how often an individual attended church. Characteristics of the listening situation that might affect critical ability included: having another person present confirm an individual's behavior, the people present, listening to the broadcast apart from one's nuclear family, immediacy of the danger, an individual's status in the group (opinion leader versus opinion follower), the disturbing effect of witnessing others' reactions, and the actual listening location (listening in a public place could mean seeing and being effected by more frightened people than at home).

In the unstable social conditions category, Cantril pointed to recent American history, including the unrest of the Great Depression, brought on by the stock market crash in 1929; fresh memories of World War I and German aggression, confusion over technological innovations (such as radio itself), the fear of another world war, and the thrill of disaster. Cantril concluded that some people wanted to believe the Martian invasion story because it provided an escape from the hassles of their ordinary, daily existence. Others, he suggested, may have been victims of suggestibility, a state of mind produced by their lack of knowledge and reasoning skills. If you link those deficiencies to fear of war and drastic economic times, Cantril wrote, you come up with an individual with little ability to resist believing a radio program that sounds like a news broadcast, and panic ensues.

To the best of their ability, using the most current social science research methods available, Cantril, Gaudet, and Herzog tracked the events of October 30, 1938, and the human reaction to them, and offered an explanation for why so many people panicked that night. Counting the appendices, *The Invasion From Mars* runs 224 pages. But, significantly, it doesn't end with their answer to the question why. Early on the authors informed readers that their goals were both scientific *and* didactic (instructional). They devoted the bulk of the text to scientific explanation. Only at the very end, with their final words, did they attempt to do a little teaching.

Perhaps with public concern over the effects of mass media in their minds, crystallized in the Magic Bullet Theory, they propose a way to prevent a radio panic like this one from ever happening again. The answer, they argue, is to help ordinary Americans (the authors prefer the term *common man*) develop the critical ability that allowed many listeners to avoid falling under the spell of the radio that night. How do we do that? Cantril offers a recipe comprised of three parts education and one part social reform. First of all, teach people to question what they see and hear, instill in them a healthy skepticism they can build on to determine what's true and what's false, what's real and what's fantastic. Then enhance their ability to examine whatever messages come at them by providing relevant knowledge. Educate them, and make sure they understand that knowledge worth having is grounded in evidence or has been tested. (Cantril's sense of what constitutes relevant knowledge sounds much like the definitions we developed in chapter one for truth, facts, and knowledge, especially in the call for testing or verifying with evidence.) Finally, to address the suggestibility that rendered so many listeners vulnerable to misunderstanding the Mercury Theatre broadcast, Cantril recommends taking steps to reduce what he calls the harassment of emotional insecurity that haunts millions of Americans who live in underprivileged environments.

Given Cantril's argument that a better-educated public will lead to a more stable society, less vulnerable to the manipulations of media messages, did America snap to attention and immediately implement his suggestions? Not right away, but there is a striking similarity between Cantril's call for critical ability and the media literacy movement, an organized educational effort that first appeared in the early 1950s, after the arrival of television. The goals of media literacy are generally compatible with Cantril's desire to empower the ordinary person to interact in a positive, constructive way with the messages delivered by mass media. In England, Canada, and Australia, media literacy is a common element in many schools. Strangely, growth of the movement in the United States has been relatively slow. Debate over how and where it should be taught has so far prevented it from becoming a standard part of the American public school curriculum. Teachers, beleaguered by externally imposed educational standards, are reluctant to surrender valuable class time to media literacy education while they struggle to prepare their classes for standardized tests. Media literacy advocates might argue that equipping our children to cope with the incredible onslaught of mass media that invades their every waking moment is every bit as important, in the long run, as test scores.

But efforts continue in the educational arena and other quarters, as well. For example, the term does not appear in the title of this book, but it is fair to say that one of the goals of this volume is to suggest ways people can accurately interpret and evaluate the subset of media messages that travel under the banner (or sometimes the guise) of news. I suspect Cantril would heartily endorse these efforts.

As for his encouragement to improve the lot of our society's underprivileged members, the current task leaves little time to explore how well we've addressed that issue. At the risk of appearing cynical, I would simply observe that America's concern for its disadvantaged has blown hot and cold over the decades since Cantril filed his report, and has seldom stopped to consider the link he established between the have-nots of our world and suggestibility, and the ultimate social consequences such a combination might produce.

Cantril entered his study of the panic whipped up by the *War of the Worlds* broadcast with the blessing of a society generally convinced, if they stopped to think about it, that modern mass media, especially film and radio, wielded a great deal of influence over human beings. The scholarly elite indicted mass media by formulating the Magic Bullet Theory, a name that carried within it a tacit admission that we didn't exactly understand how media messages affected us. (The elite would probably have used the pronoun *them* rather than *us*; they tended to think the average American was most vulnerable to whatever mass media did.) But whatever it was, the fact that they could tear into and alter our minds and emotions, our values and behaviors, in an instant, like a gunshot, meant we needed to keep a very close eye on media.

Such was the thinking when the Payne Fund decided to pay Herbert Blumer to find out what films did to our kids. The same attitudes likely prevailed in the offices of the Rockefeller Foundation when it established the Office of Radio Research at Princeton. And we've already noted that Cantril and other psychologists swarmed to mass communications research in hopes of measuring and explaining the tremendous, universal effects mass media produced in human beings, which suggests they, too, embraced the Magic Bullet Theory.

These social scientists tackled the *War of the Worlds* study expecting big confirmation of radio's big effects on listeners. They documented the panic that sent millions of people scurrying for cover or left them on their knees praying for deliverance as the end of the world approached. In their report, though, unlike in Blumer's and those who went before them, culpability for the public reaction extended beyond radio. The finger of blame also pointed straight at the audience. Cantril and his colleagues did not deny that Orson Welles's radio play served as the fuse that ignited the social explosion. But, in their attempt to answer why people panicked, the psychologists made two dramatic and potentially heretical points: not everyone who heard the broadcast was frightened by it (by some estimates, as little as a fifth of the listening audience fled into the streets, far from a majority), and those who panicked were different from those who did not (not necessarily in any outward way, but inside their heads, the ways their brains worked, their thoughts, knowledge, and attitudes.)

## Shooting Down the Magic Bullet

Bear in mind that these findings arrived when the Magic Bullet Theory reigned as *the* explanation for the impact of mass media on people. In suggesting that the *War of the Worlds* broadcast did not produce a universal effect on listeners that night, and that we could begin to predict which audience members would panic by knowing more about them as individuals, Cantril fired the first shots in a battle that would eventually topple the Magic Bullet Theory, at least among social psychologists. (To be fair, we must acknowledge that many people in the general public, and perhaps more than a few in academic circles, still harbor serious suspicions of mass media and their power to drastically affect our thoughts, values and actions.)

For our purposes in this book, Cantril's second point is most useful, his contention that he could identify characteristics in the people he interviewed that determined whether the person enjoyed an entertaining hour of radio drama the night of October 30, 1938, or experienced an apocalyptic vision of a world about to end. Those characteristics are all part of the mental and emotional preparation (their knowledge, their life experiences, their beliefs, their attitudes) that listeners brought to their encounter with the broadcast. Human beings have been using these tools for millennia; our ancient ancestors first applied them to the sights and sounds of their prehistoric world in search of understanding and meaning. We still use them in our quest for truth.

## A Map of the Mind

Today, thanks to the work of social and cognitive psychologists, we have a clearer idea of how our brain acquires and uses these elements to help us cope with the never-ending flow of life experiences, including consumption of the news. We need a basic understanding of the process of how our brains work if we hope to analyze what happens when we attempt to determine where, or if, there is Truth in the news.

We begin with a reminder that much of what we think we know about how the brain functions is based on research by scientists who, for the most part, must study their subject from a distance. Traipsing through the brain with a scalpel or a probe might produce some interesting results, but they would likely be outweighed by the physiological damage done and the ethical concerns raised by trashing the inside of someone's head. Observing changes in behaviors and capabilities after people experience brain injuries has revealed some interesting things, and the new scanning equipment we noted earlier promises to illuminate the subject further, but much of this research involves experiments that require people to use their brains to perform a variety of tasks and observing their performance. This review can't begin to do justice to the vast mountain of work already done in this area; the best we can hope for is a sketch of the most relevant facts and theories. What we need to understand, in our quest to ferret out truth from news media, is what we, in our glorious capacity as thinking, feeling human beings, bring to this mental dance that may impact what we take away from it in terms of facts, knowledge, information, opinions, and, over time, memories.

A diagram of what researchers think happens in our brain might look like this:

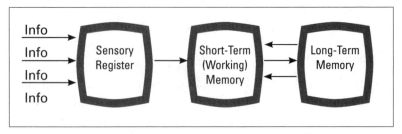

If we look at the left side of the diagram, we see arrows labeled "info" pointing toward a box labeled Sensory Register. Those arrows represent all of the sensory information available in the world around us, sights, sounds, tastes, textures, scents, or odors. Our five senses—sight, hearing, touch, taste, and smell—are designed to "read" the information they come in contact with and send a report on it, electrical impulses that travel via the nervous system, to the sensory register in the brain. Unless we suffer a disability of some kind, our senses work automatically to gather information about our world. If we open our eyes, we see; unless our ears are plugged with cotton, we hear; if we brush our hand over a piece of sandpaper, we feel. We are wonderfully made, in this sense. Keeping our sensory register chock full of sensations requires no conscious thought or effort on our part.

The sensory register holds a visual sensation very briefly, sounds "echo" in the system a bit longer. If we pay attention to these sensations, they move into the second box, Short-term or Working Memory. Researchers generally agree that if we fail to "notice" a sensation, it decays and fades from our mind. That physiological fact poses a mixed blessing. On the upside, imagine the challenge of dealing with a never-ending stream of information, especially while you're trying to focus on something else. What kind of conversation could you have with your friend while you're riding in the car if she is constantly distracted by the blur of images she sees out the window as you speed along. On the other hand, most of us have no doubt experienced the frustration of finding ourselves in a place jam-packed with visual or aural sensations we want to remember and not having enough time and attention to devote to all of them. We go away, knowing we "missed" a great deal.

When we attend to information in the sensory register, our mind sets to work trying to recognize it, understand it, and decide what it means. Psychologists call the product of this process, perceptions. The brain's principal method of forming perceptions (we are, in a sense, explaining our sensations to ourselves) is to use earlier perceptions stored in our long-term memory. The arrows pointing from Long-Term Memory to Working Memory in the diagram represent this process of calling up information already in our brains. These perceptions may be in the form of what we generally understand as facts, knowledge, beliefs, attitudes, pictures, sounds, feelings, even smells. As we mentally examine a new sensation, our mind compares it to things we've seen or heard or smelled or thought before. The result may be new perceptions or thoughts, or new information added to our existing knowledge. We don't know exactly what form these bits of information assume in the brain; some researchers talk about memory traces, a record of mental transactions, produced by electrical impulses, actually embedded in the brain's cells, that can be accessed and replayed at a later time. We store these mental products in Long-Term Memory, the last box in the diagram. This joint effort by our senses and our brain—this collection of perceptions—helps us meet our basic need for truth and understanding. Through this very natural process, we apply meaning to the experiences of our lives; we construct a sense of reality.

We can apply this information to Hadley Cantril's *War of the Worlds* study to demonstrate why understanding how our minds work is important to our efforts to find truth in the news. Much of our thinking about how we process information came after Cantril's work with the *War of the Worlds* panic. The model we've been working with, for instance, wasn't introduced until 1968. But the reasons Cantril offers for why some people panicked in 1938 certainly anticipate the point we've reached today.

As we've just noted, we now believe that our mind uses perceptions stored somewhere in our brain to process new information and decide what it means. Cantril suggests that radio listeners who came to believe they were hearing a real news report followed the same mental steps we've just outlined, but their mental resources—their memory store of past perceptions—led them to an inaccurate evaluation of what they heard. Some listeners, he suggests, had a perception (Cantril uses the term *standard of judgment*) of what a radio news bulletin sounded like that matched the broadcast, and that was enough to convince them to take it seriously. Others had no prior perception to compare the broadcast to and were uncertain how to understand what they were hearing, and that increased the likelihood they could be fooled into accepting the show as a true newscast. A third group, in Cantril's observation, had pre-existing perceptions related to radio, but they couldn't find one that fit what they were hearing that night, and they, too, fell under radio's fictional spell.

Cantril indirectly endorses the influence of pre-existing perceptions in his list of personality characteristics that inhibited audience members' ability to critically evaluate the show. People who panicked reported more insecurity, worry, and fears, and a lack of self-confidence. Many of them expressed a fatalistic

> People who panicked reported more insecurity, worry, and fears, and a lack of self-confidence. Many of them expressed a fatalistic view of life, firmly embraced a set of religious beliefs, and attended church frequently.

view of life, firmly embraced a set of religious beliefs, and attended church frequently.

Cantril's panic victims succumbed to fear partly because they lacked the knowledge they needed to properly judge the broadcast. Even some of those who appeared to have sufficient knowledge, educated people, couldn't figure it out. Their thinking, like that of many others, fell under the influence of fears, insecurities, religious beliefs, and a generally fatalistic worldview. We might be tempted to conclude that the mixture of cognitive (thought-based) and affective (emotional) experiences simply overwhelmed their ability to form realistic perceptions of the play. But a modern-day psychologist, examining Cantril's lists, might offer a much shorter explanation—attitude. And, were he alive to render an opinion, Cantril might well agree. Attitude is what the next chapter is all about.

*Chapter Three*

# Thinking about the Truth

> If you do not tell the truth about yourself you
> cannot tell it about other people.
>
> • Virginia Woolf

## It's a Question of Attitude

We have referred to attitude along the way in this exploration, even listing it as one of the mental items likely to be stored in our memory, and used, along with knowledge, to find our way through life. But, to this point, we haven't given attitudes top position in the pantheon of factors that influence our ability to process information, such as the news. Social psychologists, however, tell a different story, and it's one we need to deal with before we move on to examine journalists and the news industry. (This is a lay person's version of what's involved. Much of what follows is dealt with more extensively, and in more scholarly terms, by Alice H. Eagly and Shelly Chaiken in their very thorough volume, *The Psychology of Attitudes.*)

Long before Orson Welles adapted H. G. Wells's novel for radio, social psychologists argued that attitudes exerted a tremendous influence on human information processing. In 1935, in the *Handbook Of Social Psychology*, Gordon Allport made the point this way: "Attitudes determine for each individual what he [sic] will see and hear, what he will think, and what he will do. To borrow a phrase from William James, they 'engender meaning upon the world'; they draw lines about and segregate an otherwise chaotic environment; they are our methods for finding our way about in an ambiguous universe." If Allport is right (and modern social psychologists are still quoting him, not correcting him), we need to understand two things about attitudes before we move on—how we form them and how they affect our information processing experiences, such as reading or watching the news.

> "Attitudes . . . are our methods for finding our way about in an ambiguous universe."
> —Gordon Allport

In short, when we transfer sensations into working memory and mentally manipulate them, one of the operations our minds perform, along with trying to recognize and understand the information (whether it's a concrete object like a candy bar or an abstract object like moral values) is to judge the object and decide how we feel about it—is it good or bad, do we like it or dislike it? Researchers tell us scientific experiments prove that our attitude toward an object comprises the biggest part of the meaning we attach to it.

When a set of attitudes and beliefs develops around a social theme or issue, they form what psychologists understand as an ideology. Ideological tendencies provide labels that can be used as shorthand for describing us. Depending on our attitudes toward specific issues or policies in the political realm, for example, we might be identified as liberal or conservative.

Attitudes are an important part of the mental processes bequeathed to us by our prehistoric relatives. We are complex individuals, equipped with a virtually automatic system that allows us to move through the world collecting and evaluating information we can use to cope and survive. Attitudes allow us to quickly decide, when we encounter an object, how we should react to it. If past experience left us with a positive attitude toward the object, we can feel comfortable approaching it. If our minds retrieve a negative attitude, a sense that we don't like this thing, that it's bad, we may take steps to avoid it. The strength of an attitude, which can influence its impact on our reactions, depends on how important the issue or object is to us.

Scientists tell us attitudes can be based on feelings alone, without conscious thought. That should come as no surprise. You may recall that our feelings—what psychologists refer to as the *affective system*—are housed in the oldest part of our brain, and generated protective reflexes that helped ancient proto-humans negotiate the threats posed by the prehistoric world before they developed the ability to think.

Science also tells us that once attitudes form, they are fairly resistant to change. We may have learned that ourselves in a heated debate with someone over an issue. We think we've clearly demonstrated why their thinking is wrong, and they still depart from the conversation clinging to the exact attitudes they expressed at the beginning of the exchange. I experienced this not long ago with a family member during a Presidential campaign. We entered the election season on different sides of the political aisle, but with a fair amount of agreement on important human values and religious beliefs. In repeated conversations, over several months, I laid out what I thought were cogent, faith-based, humanitarian arguments for why my relative should come over to the other side. And my family member seemed to agree with me. I thought I had convinced her to change her attitude toward the candidates and favor mine. But just a few days before the election, she calmly informed us that she intended to vote for the candidate she originally liked best.

In instances like this, it's tempting to think of the other person as close-minded, unwilling to consider important new information that might lead her to change her attitude. But she may simply be demonstrating our natural tendency to preserve attitudes once they're formed. In a political setting, I found it frustrating. But if we think about it in the context of our day-to-day struggle to cope with a difficult and sometimes threatening world, it makes a lot of sense. My relative's political attitudes are part of her sense of reality, the system of knowledge, attitudes, and beliefs she has constructed to make sense out of the world. They are part of her Truth, and they help her get by. Psychologists defend the relative inflexibility of attitudes by suggesting that if attitudes were always subject to change, we would have a much harder time evaluating all of the information we take in each day. Making meaning out of the sensations and experiences we encounter along the way would be much more difficult because we wouldn't really know what we think about anything. In a very vital sense, scientists tell us, attitudes serve as a frame of reference for understanding and organizing all of the things, people, events, and ideas that come our way; they guide us in our need to know, our search for Truth.

## What Attitudes Are Made Of

My efforts to change an attitude might have fared better if I had paid more attention to what attitudes are made of—beliefs. In peeling the onion of attitude, scientists have discovered that most objects or sensations that we attempt to process are multifaceted. Researchers call these facets attributes. For instance, if my mind is processing an orange creamsicle, the attributes I evaluate in forming an attitude about the sweet treat might include its shape, its flavor, its color, its price, and the song the ice cream truck plays as it idles through my neighborhood. The thought or thoughts I have about each of those attributes (I believe the ice cream is orange and white, I believe it's shaped like a mitten without a thumb) will likely include an evaluation of how much I like or dislike that facet of the creamsicle. Those thoughts, with some degree of liking or disliking attached, constitute what psychologists call beliefs. According to attitude theory, all of our beliefs about an object add up to an attitude.

A major assumption of attitude research is that the judgment we make of each individual attribute (whether we like it or dislike it) tends to be consistent with our overall attitude. If all of my beliefs about the creamsicle are positive, I may hold a very strong attitude about creamsicles, I may really, really like them (which, in fact, I do). Sometimes, however, we feel positively toward some attributes of the object and negatively toward others. If we apply the mathematical model for determining attitude, we would expect that adding a mixed bag of beliefs together would produce a less extreme attitude.

You can test this theory for yourself. Think of two models of car that you like, one that you like a lot, and one that you like, but not as much. Then make a list of attributes the cars share, such as styling, performance, interior, gas mileage, value as a status symbol, environmental friendliness, power. Write down what you think about each attribute for each car, including how much you like or dislike each facet. Assign five points for each attribute, add a plus or minus sign to indicate whether you like or dislike it, and add them up. The score for the car you liked the most at the beginning of the exercise should be higher than for the car you didn't like as much.

You can use the same exercise to analyze your attitude toward people and abstract objects such as political issues or religious groups. The results may surprise you and demonstrate just how important beliefs are in determining what attitudes we hold and how extreme they are. As an example, when psychologists compared people's attitudes toward their own social group with their attitude toward a minority group they disliked, they found that the belief system that underlay people's attitude toward their own group was far more complex (they were able to admit to themselves that they liked *and* disliked things about their own group). As a result, the positive and negative beliefs tended to balance each other out and added up to an attitude toward their own group that was not so extreme. Their beliefs about the minority group, however, all tended to carry minus signs; adding those up produced a fairly extreme negative attitude toward the other group.

If we accept beliefs as the basic building blocks of attitude (and attitudes exert such a powerful influence on our perceptions of the world) we need to address the question of where beliefs come from. In chapter one, we settled on "acceptance of something as true" as an appropriate definition of belief, in a context where we're trying to discover truth in the information delivered to us by news media. We start acquiring beliefs from the moment our minds begin making meaning of the world around us. In the creamsicle example, I formed a set of beliefs about creamsicles by observing them and making judgments about the facets of them I could sense. Those thoughts produced my attitude toward creamsicles, and I stored the attitude and the beliefs in my mind as things I accepted as true about that particular object; they became part of my knowledge.

We also acquire beliefs and attitudes from those around us. Wise adults, parents, and religious leaders have known this for a long time. In a song about family relationships, rock-and-roller Graham Nash advises parents, and young people not yet parents, to teach their children well. The book of Proverbs in the Bible advises us to "train a child in the way he should go, and when he is old he will not turn from it." Science appears to confirm the writer's conviction that beliefs and attitudes learned in early years will be resistant to change later on. The accident of birth means we cannot control the attitudes and values we're exposed to early in our lives. Children generally hold the adults around them—parents, grandparents, teachers, and priests—in high regard. It seems quite natural that they would accept beliefs and attitudes taught to them by these authority figures as something that's true, especially if they have not yet acquired other knowledge or attitudes to hold up against them.

> We start acquiring beliefs from the moment our minds begin making meaning of the world around us.

The danger in this educational process, of course, lies in the fact that a free society cannot control the beliefs, attitudes, and values children learn, at home, at school, and in church. The nature of the beliefs and attitudes we teach our children, and the knowledge we neglect to provide them with, may leave them ill equipped to process some of the information they encounter later on. Teach them well, indeed. Many of the people terrified by Orson Welles's extraterrestrial attack, according to Cantril, held religious beliefs and a fatalistic worldview, most likely taught to them by their community, that prevented them from seeing the broadcast for what it was, a well-intentioned Halloween prank.

Our devotion to our beliefs, especially those most closely connected to our understanding of who we are, can make them very resistant to change, even in the face of strong evidence that the beliefs are wrong. Those beliefs can also lead us into some extreme behaviors. Witness, for instance, the long history of religious martyrs—Christian, Buddhist, Muslim, and others—whose quest for truth led them to form beliefs that convinced them to ignore their basic survival instincts and sacrifice their lives for what they perceived as a greater good.

In Jonestown, Guyana, more than 900 members of the People's Temple followed Jim Jones to the grave because they believed what he told them. Jones began preaching a message of racial inclusion and social justice in 1954 in Indiana, a state still locked in the throes of segregation. When the congregation's elders invited him to leave, he and his followers formed a new church called the People's Temple. So charismatic was Jones, that many of his members followed him to Guyana, where his increasing eccentricities eventually drew the attention of authorities back in the States. When a delegation arrived to investigate, Jones announced that the end had come and ordered his group to commit mass suicide. A total of 909 believers did.

In 1997, thirty-nine members of the Heaven's Gate cult committed suicide because they firmly believed that creatures in space ships were coming to take them to a better place. The dead ranged in age from 26 to 72, all of them believers in the doomsday rhetoric preached by Marshall Applewhite and Bonnie Nettles. Cult members feared persecution, death, and arrest if they remained on earth. They believed their salvation would arrive in the form of a UFO traveling in the tail of the Hale-Bopp comet.

> Cult members feared persecution, death, and arrest if they remained on earth. They believed their salvation would arrive in the form of a UFO traveling in the tail of the Hale-Bopp comet.

Nearly eighty people followed David Koresh, a self-professed angel and agent of God, to Waco, Texas, and died in a fiery confrontation with federal agents, because they believed what Koresh told them. Shortly before the fire, I interviewed a father who had just rescued his teenage daughter from Koresh's compound after learning that Koresh planned to make her one of his wives. The girl's mother, a devout disciple, remained with Koresh and died in the blaze. When I asked how his former wife came to have faith in David Koresh, the man told me her lengthy spiritual quest led her to Waco in search of a higher truth. She so devoutly believed what she was told there that no argument could change her mind. Her resistance cost her her life.

## Who Ya Gonna Believe?

Psychologists tell us we can learn beliefs and attitudes directly or indirectly, and again, depending on our perceptions of that information, the results may be socially unfortunate. Racial prejudice, for example, which psychologists consider the sum of a set of negative beliefs, is a learned attitude. And, at the risk of turning this discussion into a confessional, I'm living proof that it can be formed from both direct and indirect instruction in beliefs about people of color.

My parents seldom, if ever, used the word "nigger" in front of me when I was a child (although I do remember adults telling jokes that ended with a punch line and a laugh delivered at the expense of people of color). During the civil rights era, my folks sometimes pointed out that their country school was integrated long before legislative efforts began to require it. They would have insisted they had no prejudice against people of color. They did refer to them as "colored people," and I occasionally heard my father express disgust over African-Americans living on welfare while the rest of us toiled at low-paying jobs to make ends meet.

But much of my education about African-Americans, the information that produced my racial beliefs and attitudes, was indirect. No black people lived in our small town, although my friend's mother hired a black woman to clean her house. (The explanation we learned as children was that blacks could work in town, but they could not rent an apartment or own a house.) In the summer, a wonderful woman from the community came to my church to teach Sunday school for the grown-ups and the kids. She used puppets and told interesting stories. Given the times (integration was a hot topic), she addressed the racial issue in metaphorical terms, basically preaching segregation. One of her stories included the line, "You never see a blackbird in a robin's nest." I can't be sure if they really did, but in my memory I see the adults in that Sunday school room, people I loved and respected and look to for input as I sought truth with which to construct my sense of reality, nodding and smiling in agreement. I remember my mother repeating that line to me years later when, as a would-be college intellectual, I broached the subject of interracial marriage.

One of the strongest indirect influences on my attitudes toward people of color was a family trip to Washington, D.C., when I was about ten years old. On the way to one of the monuments (for dramatic purposes it's tempting to remember it was the Lincoln Memorial) we took a wrong turn and suddenly found ourselves in a neighborhood where all the people in the cars, on the sidewalks, and on the porches were black. I don't remember thinking much about it until my mother turned to my brother and me in the back seat and, with slight urgency, told us to roll up our windows and lock our doors. She didn't say anything else, and my father soon had us out of the neighborhood and headed toward our destination. The only thing that had changed when we turned the corner was the skin color of the people outside our car. Instructions to roll up windows and lock doors told me the people outside must pose some threat to us. It was clear that my mother believed these people might harm us, although they seemed to be paying little attention to us. The conclusion I reached, as a little white boy growing up in a white world, was that black people are to be feared. The collective beliefs I had come to accept as true about people of color added up to a negative attitude, prejudice.

Looking back, it's startling to realize that I formed this negative racial attitude at the same time the crusade for civil rights and equality was gathering strength and spilling into America's streets. I am embarrassed, if not ashamed, how little awareness I had of the movement and leaders like Rosa Parks and Martin Luther King. I don't remember my high school teachers encouraging us to think about such things. In my church and community, if news media raised the subject, I remember hearing adults denounce demonstrations and marches, condemn riots, and state, in no uncertain terms, that American blacks had forgotten their place. The adults around me protected and reinforced my bigotry.

But that protection did not extend to my college biology class a couple of years later. Although many on campus endorsed segregation and other symbols of racial prejudice (the school operated under the watchful eye of a fundamentalist Christian denomination), my science professor still managed to construct a syllabus that required us to read the latest discoveries related to genetics and race. The bottom line, according to our text, was that the long-established concept of race, so central in building negative attitudes toward minority groups, really provided little scientific support for prejudice. Arguments that people of color were inherently inferior to whites had to deal with the discovery that what we called "race" was no more than skin deep. From a genetic perspective, every human being on earth is essentially the same, with minor differences such as the color of our skin or the shape of our nose dictated by information embedded deep in our cells, information that, depending on our parentage, might be translated into features in any of us.

This information, so familiar to many of us today, slammed into my racist attitudes like the proverbial ton of bricks. My long-established beliefs about blacks told me they were inferior to whites and possibly even dangerous. Now, these scientists were telling me that was not true. I experienced a fairly intense amount of psychological discomfort in the moment (scientists call it cognitive dissonance) and my reaction to it introduces another important aspect of attitudes and beliefs—they can change.

## The Throb of Cognitive Dissonance

Scientists believe that along with our natural human tendency to gather information about our world and pass judgment on it—the process of making meaning out of our sensations and constructing a sense of reality—we have a natural desire for peace of mind; psychologists refer to it as psychological comfort or equilibrium. When we encounter information that clashes with the system of knowledge and attitudes we've put together, we experience a sort of mental pain and confusion, which interferes with our ongoing information processing. And, not so differently from the way we would react if someone repeatedly poked us in the stomach with a stick, we look for ways to reduce or eliminate the discomfort in our brain.

One way to reduce the discomfort caused by conflicting attitudes is to think of more beliefs that support our original attitude. In a sense, we're loading the scales in favor of what we thought in the first place. In my biology class experience, as an example, I might look to people whose beliefs I respect for arguments that dismiss genetic research. One of my classmates once told me, for instance, that blacks can't digest dairy products, which would mean their digestive systems differ from ours, which would refute the assertion that racial differences are only skin deep. Some of the faculty and students at my college believed that the Bible and God have established that blacks are subordinate to whites. Thomas Jefferson and Abraham Lincoln are both said to have believed that black intelligence, generally, functioned beneath that of whites. If I accepted these beliefs as true, I could "bolster" my prejudice and restore my psychological equilibrium.

That's not what happened to me. In the face of information from a source that I respected (scientific research), information that was incongruent with information and attitudes communicated to me by people I loved and respected, I found myself with a serious case of cognitive dissonance. Unable to argue the genetic information away, I experienced intense psychological discomfort. Psychologists might illustrate my mental dilemma this way:

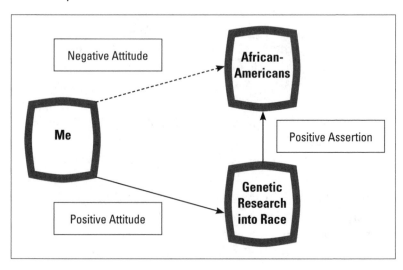

In the diagram, the dotted line represents my negative attitude toward people of color, my racial prejudice. The solid line between "Me" and "Genetic Research into Race" indicates my positive attitude toward scientific research. The solid line between Genetic Research into Race and African-Americans represents the positive assertion, based on scientific study, that all human beings are essentially alike and equal, regardless of minor differences like skin color. I experienced cognitive dissonance because the positive statement about people of color conflicted with the negative view of black people I learned growing up. I liked research but I didn't like blacks, and the fact that science held an opposing attitude toward people of color caused me mental pain.

When we confront this sort of psychological conflict, if bolstering our existing attitude doesn't work, the mind very cleverly finds anther way to reduce the discomfort; we change one or more of our attitudes and beliefs, and restore peace of mind. Which one we change depends on a number of factors, including how long and how deeply we've held an attitude and how we feel about the person who introduces the conflicting attitude. The tendency, according to scientists, is to change the attitude that most conflicts with our established beliefs. Given my past experience, that should have meant adopting a more negative attitude toward science and no longer accepting the findings of genetic research as the truth. If that happened, my racist attitudes would most likely have become more extreme.

I am happy to report that, perhaps by the grace of God, that is not what happened. Because I embraced my belief in the power of science to explain the world to us more deeply than I did the beliefs about race communicated to me, largely indirectly, by the adults around me during my formative years (beliefs and attitudes often not accompanied by clear, rational arguments), I changed my attitude about people of color to one based on what I believed to be the truth of science. Establishing positive attitudes toward science and toward people of color reduced my mental discomfort.

My new attitude toward blacks also fit more closely with other beliefs taught to me in church, especially in songs like "Jesus Loves Me," with lyrics that informed me that Jesus loves all of the children in the world, regardless of the color of their skin. As I thought about my new attitude, and my mind pulled up all of the racial beliefs I had stored away over the years, I realized that much of my religious instruction clashed with the racist attitudes passed on to me by my society, including adults who were part of my religious education. As a child, I hadn't seen the contradictions and hadn't experienced any cognitive dissonance as I added them to my memory bank. Now, as an emerging adult, working to attach my own meaning to reality apart from that instilled in me by my parents and my community, and with the encouragement of enlightened college faculty, I readily suffered the psychological discomfort that resulted from examining my existing attitudes and beliefs in light of new information (that's probably overstating the case, it wasn't always pleasant to reach the conclusion that adults I loved and respected held attitudes I now viewed as unfair or destructive). But I persevered because, I believe, the process is an integral part of our basic drive to know the Truth about existence. For me, the honest quest for truth, wherever it can be found, is a large part of what it means to be truly human.

> I realized that much of my religious instruction clashed with the racist attitudes passed on to me by my society, including adults who were part of my religious education.

Cognitive dissonance can also flare up and cause us to change our attitudes as we process messages from news media. One of the best examples occurred in 1968, as the Democratic Party was nominating its presidential candidate in Chicago. You may recall reports of that convention; you may have been in Chicago that summer. Student activists filled the streets to protest, among other things, the Vietnam War. Live television coverage allowed the nation to watch as the demonstrators clashed with police. Then the violence moved inside the convention itself. As CBS correspondent Dan Rather attempted to interview delegates on the crowded convention floor, viewers saw him knocked to the ground, apparently by security forces assigned there by the city of Chicago and its mayor, Richard Daley.

At the CBS anchor desk that night, looking on with the rest of the audience, was Walter Cronkite, a journalist toward whom many Americans held a strong, positive attitude. (Viewers liked and respected Cronkite so much that, in a poll four years later, he easily outstripped the leading political figures of the day to claim the title "Most Trusted Man in America.") As Rather went down, Cronkite observed that a "bunch of thugs" seemed to be controlling the convention. Bearing in mind our discussion of cognitive dissonance, and factoring in the apparent fact that many audience members, especially in Chicago, held very positive attitudes toward Mayor Daley and his police force, you can probably predict which way the tide of public reaction ran. To relieve the cognitive dissonance created when Cronkite (a person they liked and respected) expressed a seriously negative attitude toward Mayor Daley and the police (people viewers also held in high esteem), many people in the audience traded in their positive attitude toward Cronkite for a negative one. Deciding they didn't like Cronkite and CBS made it easier for them to deal with Cronkite's negative attitude toward the mayor and the cops. Viewers broadcast their reconstructed attitude in a flood of critical calls and letters to CBS.

A few years later, media coverage of the events surrounding Richard Nixon's final weeks as President generated significant cognitive dissonance for an elderly member of our family. A well-educated person, she grew up in a generation of Americans who held very positive attitudes, including a high degree of trust and respect, toward the office of the President and whoever held that important position. She also held a positive attitude toward news media and trusted them as a source of truth. As the Watergate Hearings unfolded, and TV news began delivering very negative messages about the President's behavior, our family member suffered severe psychological discomfort. Her positive attitude toward the President clashed with the news delivered by the media, about whom she also held a positive attitude. If she was to restore peace of mind, one of those attitudes had to change. For those of us in the post-Watergate era, the decision might go either way. For this senior citizen's generation, with their long-held, deeply rooted belief in the goodness of the Presidency, the choice was clear. After listening to the beginning of the litany of wrongdoings charged to Richard Nixon and his administration, she informed the family that the news media shouldn't treat the President in such a disrespectful way and that she rejected their allegations. With that, she left the TV room. She stayed away for the duration of the hearings, only to return after President Ford pardoned Nixon for his transgressions. With her lifelong faith in the Presidency and her recently formed distrust of the media firmly intact, she returned to the family room and triumphantly announced, "See, I told you the President was innocent."

The convention story and my relative's experience with news media illustrate the negative impact of cognitive dissonance. My experience with racial attitudes suggests that a little psychological discomfort can produce a change for the better. In my case, it happened almost accidentally, a chance encounter with information that forced me to reconsider what I believed. But I think we could accomplish some very positive things by intentionally capitalizing on our natural tendency to reduce psychological discomfort.

As an example, I would cite a television program I proposed years ago designed to benefit hearing-impaired children. These children generally have low self-esteem, a poor opinion of themselves. My goal in the show was to generate cognitive dissonance

for these kids that would push their self-esteem in a positive direction. To do it, I proposed producing a show for these children
with actor Lou Ferrigno as the host. In those days, Ferrigno was
known to millions of kids as the Incredible Hulk. It is an under-
statement to say that children held a positive attitude toward
The Hulk; they loved the guy. What many hearing-impaired
kids didn't know was that Ferrigno achieved his success as a
super hero in spite of a serious hearing disability. I hoped to
create some psychological discomfort for these kids by having
Ferrigno reveal his disability during the program, and then let
them know that he still felt very good about himself and his ac-
complishments. The kids' negative attitude toward themselves
as hearing-impaired persons and their positive attitude toward
Ferrigno should set them up for some mental distress when
they learn that their attitude toward the hearing-impaired (including themselves) clashed with their hero's. My hope was that
the children would opt to retain their attitude toward Ferrigno
and ease their mental pain by deciding it was alright to feel
good about themselves, too. I called the program *Candoo*, to
reinforce the positive vibes Ferrigno delivered about his life
as a hearing-impaired person. The idea drew some positive
feedback, but I regret that the show never found its way onto
videotape.

Mass media producers, especially in television, have been
using cognitive dissonance to raise awareness and encourage
changes in our attitudes and behaviors for years. Norman Lear
created the popular sitcom *All in the Family* to show us what
bigotry looks like, in hopes that cognitive dissonance would
lead us to revise racist attitudes. Writers have added an ever-
widening variety of minority groups (ethnic and sexual) to
their casts, partly to attract audience, but partly to encourage
more tolerant attitudes, as well. Cognitive dissonance plays a
role in public service announcements created for the war on
drugs and in campaigns the cable industry has mounted to promote parental control of TV.

## Tuning out Discomfort

The mental effort involved in changing our attitudes to reduce the discomfort of cognitive dissonance can make us more than a little gun-shy about encountering it at all. If we experience enough of it, we naturally begin looking for ways to avoid it. The name psychologists apply to these dissonance-avoiding tactics is selectivity, and as Allport suggested in 1935, attitudes play a huge part in the process.

Allport contended that attitudes have a tremendous influence on what we see and hear and think about. When we engage in selectivity to avoid cognitive dissonance, we filter all of the sensations and information delivered by our senses through our existing knowledge, attitudes, and beliefs, and make mental decisions about how to deal with them. Those decisions determine whether or not we will process the information, how we will understand the information, and how well we will remember the information. Psychologists refer to these three filters as selective exposure, selective perception, and selective retention or memory. Let's take a brief look at how each one works.

Psychologists believe we set the stage for selective exposure the moment we form an attitude toward something or someone. Later, if we perceive that we're about to encounter information that conflicts with our attitude (an experience we know will generate cognitive dissonance), we may take steps to avoid being exposed to it and having to think about it. If we choose to change the channel the moment we see Jerry Springer on our TV screen, we're probably engaging in selective exposure. Our moral values (attitudes toward abstract objects) may clash with the messages we expect to encounter if we watch the program. We can also avoid mental discomfort if we choose to expose ourselves to information and experiences that we suspect will agree with the attitudes we've already formed. Past experience may have taught us that reading *National Review* preserves our peace of mind far better than reading *The Nation*.

Selective perception involves information we've decided to process and attach meaning to, information we're willing to think about. If our senses deliver new information that comes close to what we already know or believe, but some aspect of it rubs against our existing attitude, our mind may detect potential psychological discomfort. To head off cognitive dissonance, we may convince ourselves that this new information fits our beliefs more closely than it really does. For example, social scientists have found that if we commit ourselves to a political candidate (because we like her), and then discover that she favors some issues we don't, our minds will tell us that our views match hers more than they actually do; we adjust our perception of what she means in order to preserve our initial attitude.

If our initial perception tells us that a statement we've just taken in clashes with attitudes we already hold, we may move to defuse any persuasive power the message has by telling ourselves that the entire statement is less like our existing attitude than it really is. At that point, we can reject the statement and get on with believing what we already believe. Imagine, for instance, what might happen to the communication process when an antiwar demonstrator confronts a war veteran. If the protestor argues that war is immoral, the vet may well "hear" himself being called a murderer, even though the demonstrator didn't actually say that. For the veteran, who holds a positive attitude toward military action and his involvement in it, attaching a more extreme meaning to the incoming message makes it easier to reject.

Selective perception allows us to slot information into two basic categories, biased and unbiased. If we decide the meaning of the message fits what we already think, we see it as fair and unbiased. If we perceive the meaning to conflict with our pre-existing knowledge and attitudes, we dismiss it as unfair and biased. Selective perception helps us preserve peace of mind, but it also poses a serious challenge if we are honestly and sincerely seeking the Truth.

The selectivity process also operates on our memory. Scientists suggest that information we store that is consistent with our beliefs and attitudes may be easier to remember. We may repress information that conflicts with our beliefs. If we end up storing information that caused cognitive dissonance when we first encountered it, we may tend to forget or distort the troublesome parts when we recall the information and think about it later on. Information that clashes with our existing attitudes may be harder to connect to what we already think and know, and weak connections could make the information harder to find later.

Selective memory, influenced by our attitudes, may bias our ability to reconstruct accurate memories of objects, ideas, and experiences. It's not exactly intentional. It's just our mind trying to fill the gaps in what we are able to remember. If our memory can't supply the complete picture, our mind taps our store of knowledge and attitudes and fills in the blanks using information that seems to fit the situation. The memory reported to our conscious mind may not be an exact match for the information we originally took in. Reporters need to keep this in mind as they canvas a crime scene trying to reconstruct what actually happened. Police are increasingly aware of the unreliability of memory. It's made them more leery of building too much of their case against a defendant on eyewitnesses.

Researchers have even cast doubt on the reliability of flash bulb memories, those pictures and sounds and ideas connected to some dramatic or emotional moment that we *think* are etched indelibly into our brain. A study of people's memory of the tragic 1986 Challenger space shuttle explosion, a shocking event that surely triggered a flash bulb moment for many of us, showed that after two years many people couldn't accurately recall where they were when they first learned of the accident. The same is probably true for many of us if we try to remember details of the moment we first learned that terrorists had crashed airplanes into the World Trade Center towers in New York in 2001. The hazards of reconstructed memory are very familiar to any journalist who covers traffic accidents. Five different witnesses may tell five different stories, which makes it very hard to report the *truth* about the crash.

## So Where Are We?

By this point, the connection between the way our minds deal with the endless flow of information gathered by our senses and our attempt to find truth in the news may be obvious. I hope so; I think it's essential to be aware of the processes involved as we launch an examination of the news and the people who deliver it to us. For the sake of clarity, let me try to pull it all together.

As human beings we share a natural drive to understand the world in which we find ourselves, at least enough to survive. To serve that need, we have developed the ability to gather a vast array of information about the world (through our senses) and process it (think about and evaluate it) in our minds. The end product is a store of knowledge and attitudes that help us know what to think, say, and do when we encounter people, places, and things as we move through our lives. Knowledge and attitudes are built on beliefs (secular and religious), things we accept as true about the world, ourselves, and the nature of human existence.

All of this processing and storing allows us to construct a sense of reality, an explanation of how it all works. Our sense of reality may be similar to someone else's if the place we live and the things we're taught are the same, but because it's built from our personal reaction to our experiences, it is also unique, as each of us is born with a unique personality. And because we rely on our sense of reality (our set of knowledge, attitudes, and beliefs) to survive physically and socially, we resist efforts to change the way we think, so much so that when an opposing view or belief finds its way into our mind, we experience mental discomfort (cognitive dissonance). To reduce that discomfort and restore our peace of mind, we have developed a natural tendency to avoid troubling information or we fiddle with its meaning to make it less threatening. Sometimes, depending on the nature of the information or where it came from, we may even change our attitudes or beliefs. If we manage to make what we think or believe more like the dissonant information or make the dissonant information more like what we already believe, the cognitive dissonance fades, and we feel better.

In our ongoing encounter with the world, attitudes and beliefs play a critical role. They influence how we process information and even help us decide what information to process. And that fact brings us to the central point of this section: If we accept the view that we naturally seek information that will allow us to understand reality and survive in the world, it's no surprise that we are attracted to the news, which purports, at least, to provide us with some of the information we need. We are, as Shoemaker phrases it, hard-wired for it. But we are also hard-wired to approach the news as we approach any other information. We take it in through our attitudes and beliefs and it is subject to our natural tendency to be selective about the information we're exposed to, what meaning we attach to it, and how accurately we remember it. In practice, that means we might opt to avoid news we suspect will conflict with what we already believe, or we might, almost without realizing it, seek news that fits what we already think. To use the old metaphor of "preaching to the choir," our attitudes and beliefs determine which choir we sit in, and we select a preacher whose sermon will be most comforting and reassuring to us.

### Who's Biased?

The basic nature of our mental life means we will evaluate whatever news we're exposed to by filtering it through what we think we know and what we know we believe. Our tendency will be to decide that news reports similar to our attitudes are fair and unbiased; stories that conflict with or challenge our beliefs may strike us as unfair and biased. We are quick to accuse news media of foisting slanted information on the public. (Many of those charges may be well-founded; journalists, after all, are human beings subject to the same natural tendencies as the rest of us. We'll examine that issue more closely in chapter five.) But, given what we think we know about how the mind works, how objective are we as we process the news?

Objectivity involves a fair and open consideration of information without any influence from our emotions or prejudices. But our mind, wondrous mechanism that it is, comes with built-in biases—our attitudes and beliefs—that exert tremendous influence on perceptions we form of any information. In the face of that fact, we might be tempted to give up before we've even tried to give new information a fair hearing. I've often heard people, including journalists, say that human beings simply can't be objective, the combined influence of all the things we think and know and feel is too great. And some of us, who believe we have nothing else to learn, who live in the certainty that our knowledge, attitudes, and beliefs are based on absolute Truth and cannot and should not be changed, may be content to have the conversation stop right there.

But our thoughts and perceptions need not be captive to what's already in our heads. If we believe that objectivity is a useful tool in the search for truth, we can work at achieving a greater sense of open-mindedness to other ways of seeing the world. Yes, we are inclined by nature and the accident of birth to form and cling to a certain set of views. They are part and parcel of the sense of reality we begin constructing almost from the moment we're born. And having

> Our mind, wondrous mechanism that it is, comes with built-in biases—our attitudes and beliefs—that exert tremendous influence on perceptions we form of any information.

them in place gives us a certain sense of security. We have examined the world around us and been taught to believe certain things. Opening up those attitudes and beliefs to scrutiny may feel risky to us. But I believe it's a risk well worth taking. If we reexamine what we've learned along the way and are willing to make adjustments in our attitudes and form new attitudes, we can strengthen our sense of reality, improve communication, and draw closer to the rest of humanity.

## Checking What's on the Shelves

We can start by taking stock of our current attitudes and beliefs. This would involve more than simply listing them. Psychologists have found that thinking about our existing attitudes without examining them may encourage us to add more supporting beliefs to them and may leave them more firmly entrenched, decreasing the chances that we could give fair consideration to a contradictory idea.

One exercise psychologists recommend to increase objectivity and openness is directed thinking. I like to think of this as the Atticus Finch approach. In Harper Lee's classic novel, *To Kill a Mockingbird*, Atticus gives his young daughter, Jem, some advice on how to get along with people who don't think about things the way she does. He tells her, "You never really understand a person until you consider things from his point of view . . . until you climb into his skin and walk around in it." In directed thinking, we force ourselves to think someone else's thoughts; we walk around in their skin and try to look at the world as they do. You may be thinking: "Beware cognitive dissonance!" And that may be one result. But psychologists tell us this sort of activity may also result in a less extreme attitude toward a person or idea than we held before. A more moderate attitude might reduce our tendency to engage in selective perception and improve our ability to process related information and attitudes. In short, we have a better chance of approaching information, like the news, in a more objective way. As we move toward objectivity, the meaning we attach to a news story should more closely match the meaning the reporter intended to communicate. If we have an accurate perception of the message we can make a better decision about whether or not it carries truth for us.

Directed thinking isn't easy. It takes work, as does objectivity. In a sense, as we've already seen, both practices tend to run against human nature. I suspect most of us can remember moments when we wanted to view some event in an open-minded way and had a tough time pulling it off. Televised political debates can be especially trying occasions. When the dust settles, we are inclined to decide the candidate we like best won, even if the post-debate experts give her performance a drubbing. A popular example of this happening on a large scale is the first televised Presidential debate, in 1960, between Richard Nixon and John F. Kennedy. Most debate gurus concede that Nixon did a better job of discussing the issues. But most of the people in the TV audience sided with Kennedy. Why? Because Kennedy looked tanned and relaxed on TV, while Nixon refused to use makeup and suffered from a flood of perspiration that streamed down his upper lip. Viewers evaluated what they saw and heard from the candidates and formed a more positive attitude toward the Senator from Massachusetts. They just liked him better. Chances are most audience members never stopped to realize they picked a winner based on feelings (attitude) rather than on an objective analysis of the thoughts expressed by the candidates.

I ran head-on into the effect of attitudes repeatedly during my years as a reporter, especially when I was assigned to cover events related to the ongoing debate over abortion. Attitudes toward the issue were extremely polarized in our community, as they are in much of our country. When the anniversary of

*Roe v. Wade* rolled around, and both sides staged demonstrations in support of their views, I always tried to ignore my personal attitude on the issue and submit a story that gave the opposing positions equal time. In spite of my best effort and good intentions, both camps usually accused me of biased reporting. Given the extremity of the attitudes on both sides, I shouldn't have been surprised that they made little effort to approach my story with the same objectivity I tried to bring to the process of writing it.

Another way to get in touch with our attitudes and beliefs, without feeling like we're throwing the door open and sweeping out our carefully constructed sense of reality, is to spend some time thinking about how we would defend what psychologists refer to as cultural truisms—truths (both religious and secular) so widely held, at least in the corner of the world where we choose to live, that they're seldom challenged. These are the core values or attitudes on which we base our understanding of ourselves and of how the world works.

The great English writer John Milton endorsed this exercise. He firmly believed that the best way to establish the truth was by testing what we believe against other ideas and values. Milton had little tolerance for psychological protection tactics like selective exposure. In an appeal to Parliament not to censor publication of unorthodox ideas (entitled *Areopagitica*), he wrote: "I cannot praise a fugitive and cloistered virtue, unexercised and unbreathed, that never sallies out and sees her adversary but slinks out of the race." Milton wasn't attacking the accepted values and beliefs of his day. On the contrary, he wanted to help us strengthen our attitudes by holding them up against ideas that challenged them. He knew, intuitively, that untested ideology and beliefs are vulnerable to strong persuasive messages delivered by powerful, charismatic individuals. And social science supports him. Psychologists tell us that if we confront conflicting beliefs and attitudes directly and develop arguments that refute them, and then store all of that information in our memory, our original attitude will be more resistant when it faces challenging perspectives and highly persuasive counterarguments in the future.

I think there may be a side effect of this process that can contribute to our ability to approach ideas and information, including the news, more objectively. To develop valid arguments against new information we must clearly understand our own attitudes *and* the ideas raised against them. We might well experience one of those "Ah ha!" moments, when we discover some truth or learn a new fact we had not known before. In the end, an exercise begun as a way to shore up our existing attitudes might end up teaching us something new about an issue, a value, or ourselves.

Examining our attitudes, dissecting our prejudices, and engaging in exercises like directed thinking should increase our ability to objectively process the news. These exercises might also improve our ability to discriminate among the vast array of news sources available in our mass mediated world. We may begin to ask more questions about the information they deliver and about the attitudes and beliefs held by those who deliver it. Where did they get the news they report? What, if any, axe do they have to grind? What factors, in addition to attitudes, beliefs, and knowledge, influence the way journalists do their jobs? Are they, in fact, a valid source of truth? If that happens, we will be well on our way to developing the critical ability Hadley Cantril believed was vital for human beings facing the power of mass media.

It's no breaking story to report that today's news professionals are under fire from just about every direction—the public, politicians, and even their own colleagues. Poll results indicate that journalists have slipped a long way from the day when TV news anchor Walter Cronkite ranked as the most trusted man in America. Critics now accuse news media of being biased, deceitful, sensational, superficial, overly commercial, immoral, arrogant, and just about anything but truthful. If the charges are valid, sifting through the news in an objective search for truth amounts to an exercise in futility. To find out whether or not our efforts are in vain, let's take a close look at the state of the news in our day.

# Chapter Four

# The Public Challenge: Truth-Telling in Journalism History

The facts fairly and honestly presented; truth will take care of itself.

■ William Allen White

Love them or hate them, journalists have been around, in one form or another, for a very long time. In a sense, they grew naturally out of our inherent need to know. In very early times, religious leaders, storytellers and wandering poets helped keep us informed, mingling society's myths (its deepest truths) and current events in verse and song. The ancient Romans introduced a more systematic approach. As early as 131 B.C.E., they posted official reports of military, municipal, legal and political developments, on stone and metal tablets, for citizens to read. Some historians consider these accounts the earliest foray into news publishing. Much like today, the fledgling journalists assigned to publish this information apparently had their critics; Roman authorities eventually censored news from the political beat (*Acta senatus*). Storytelling, songs, poems, and Roman "newspapers" served an important function in keeping the public informed, but they had limited reach, a deficiency that time and technology would remedy.

In relatively rapid sequence, beginning in the mid-sixteenth century, the printing press, steam power, electricity, radio, television, and computers, along with the spread of literacy to the lower classes dramatically increased reporters' ability to inform the masses. When the word "news" first entered the English language around 1500, it simply meant a report of recent events, most likely delivered in person. Today, "the news" is a multi-billion dollar global industry pumping out more information than we can begin to process.

Public opinion of the news has plummeted at times over the centuries, but our need for information keeps us coming back for more. Thanks to The Project for Excellence in Journalism at Columbia University we have a fairly clear idea of what the American mass media audience and the news business looked like in 2004. First of all, even though we heard a lot about declining circulation in the newspaper business, sixty percent of the more than 296 million people in the U.S. still read the paper regularly. The Big Three broadcast television networks (ABC, CBS, NBC) have lost ground with the advent of cable, satellite, and the Internet, but they still reach more than twenty-eight million people, on average, with their evening news programs. Cable news (CNN, MSNBC, Fox News) attracts a combined nightly audience of more than two-and-a-half million people. Radio has lost some of its audience to other media, but more than ninety-four percent of Americans report that they listen to radio news each week. And the new kid on the block, Internet news, already attracts an estimated ninety-two million adult information seekers regularly, that's nearly three-quarters of all Americans who are online.

> Public opinion of the news has plummeted at times over the centuries, but our need for information keeps us coming back for more.

As it has from the beginning, delivering information to all of those people costs money. Whether their source is print or broadcast or computer-driven, those millions of Americans wouldn't be able to indulge their surveillance drive if news companies couldn't make a buck or two providing it. Not to worry. News has become a major cash cow. Revenue from advertising brought newspapers a combined total of thirty-three billion dollars in 2004, according to the Newspaper Association of America. In 2003, the Big Three TV networks sold more than 463 million dollars in advertising time on their evening news shows alone. Cable news profits totaled nearly 640 million dollars in 2003. The top one hundred local television stations topped more than thirteen billion dollars in revenue in 2004, according to the TV Bureau of Advertising. And the big three weekly news-magazines (*Time, Newsweek, U.S. News & World Report*) and America's radio stations (especially those with news/talk formats) both saw their advertising revenue rise in 2004.

In a nutshell, news is big business, very big. And that has attracted big corporations, who, thanks to generous owner-ship laws in the United States, have been lassoing dozens of individual news organizations (newspapers, websites, radio and television stations, broadcast and cable news networks) and corralling them under centralized management designed to maximize how much milk these cash cows produce. That's not meant to be a criticism. It's simply part of the reality of the news business today. From an economic standpoint it's a sensible thing to do, and it shouldn't have any effect on a journalist's ability to tell the truth.

But voices inside and outside the news industry suggest that sometimes it does. Award-winning science reporter Laurie Garrett was inside at *Newsday*, but she's outside now, partly because she found more interesting work, but also because she believes the focus on the bottom line has diminished her news-paper's commitment to telling the truth. When she left *Newsday* in 2005, the International Labor Communications Association website published her farewell memo to co-workers. In it, she lamented the corporate takeover of the news and said "the drive for higher share prices and push for larger dividend returns trumps everything that the grunts in the newsroom consider their mission. . . . The sort of in-your-face challenge that the

Fourth Estate once posed for politicians has been replaced by mudslinging, lies and, where it ought not be, timidity. When I started out in journalism, the newsrooms were still full of old guys with blue collar backgrounds who became genuinely indignant when the governor lied or somebody turned off the heat on a poor person's apartment in mid-January."

It's not uncommon to hear journalists with more than a few miles on their Rolodex recall, with apparent sincerity, a time when news work and news workers were different. If that's true and if working in that environment instilled in them a commitment to discovering and reporting the truth, good for them and, in the end, good for us. But even back in that day, somebody owned the paper those blue-collar, straight-from-the-shoulder reporters worked for. Did their publishers simply sit back and watch their staffs take on evildoers? Is it possible that the attitudes some journalists have formed today in response to corporate ownership of mass media are leading them to engage in a bit of selective memory? Is what they remember an accurate reflection of what it was really like back then? Perhaps a brief look at American journalism history will help us answer those questions.

## How It Used To Be

Students of journalism, especially First Amendment advocates, are fond of quoting reporter A. J. Liebling's observation that "freedom of the press is limited to those who own one." The history of news reporting in the United States is built largely on private ownership. The earliest publications resembling a newspaper were put out by early-eighteenth-century printers, business people who owned printing presses, who discovered they could make money by publishing and selling business, political, and social information, mostly to other business people and government officials. (Common people couldn't afford the paper and most of them couldn't have read it if they had bought one.) The King of England still controlled the colonies in those days and most printers avoided publishing information that might offend the powers that be. Trying to tell the truth in a way not sanctioned by the Crown could result in legal problems and jeopardize a printer's livelihood. This was not in-your-face journalism.

But there were some bright moments for the truth squad. Over time, colonial merchants and other professionals, including some newspaper publishers, began to chafe under what they saw as England's increasingly oppressive attempts to control them and their businesses from a royal court three thousand miles away. One newspaper, in particular, began publishing critical, but accurate, stories about the royally appointed Governor of New York. Naturally, the governor was offended by the news. He charged the editor, John Peter Zenger, with sedition. The colonial jury chosen to hear the case was having none of that; they sided with Zenger. At first glance that may not strike us as terribly significant, given that the jury was composed mostly of Zenger's peers. But the acquittal becomes a journalistic landmark when we learn that it was based on the jury's belief that, even in the King's colonies, newspapers should have the right to publish information critical of public officials, as long as it's true. The decision laid the foundation for the freedom of speech that would later be listed first in the Bill of Rights guaranteed to us by the Constitution.

It would be nice to report that the Zenger case ushered in an age of objective and truthful journalism in America that has prevailed to the present day. Most versions of American journalistic history agree it did not. Loyalist publishers remained loyal, printing news with an attitude that suited the King's court. They had two important reasons for doing so: reporting the news from the Crown's point of view kept them out of jail and loyalist subscribers (the only source of income from newspapering at the time) threatened to stop buying the paper if it caused them cognitive dissonance. Of course, they didn't actually say that, but it's a good bet they weren't looking to the newspaper to disrupt their peace of mind.

While loyalist publishers maintained the royal status quo, a new brand of journalism sprang up alongside them. The leaders of the patriot movement, mostly business people, leaned on sympathetic publishers to print news that would attract the working class (a potential source of soldiers if it came to war) to their crusade to get the King's hand out of their pocket. The movement's leaders, including Sam Adams, didn't expect understaffed publishers to haul the freight alone. They hit the street as correspondents and submitted the *Journal of Occurrences*, a collection of reports accusing British soldiers stationed in Boston of abusing colonial men and violating colonial women. Royal officials denied the charges and denounced the journalists. The Governor of New York reportedly informed his superiors "if the Devil himself was of the party . . . there could not have been got together a greater collection of impudent, virulent, and seditious lies, perversions of truth, and misrepresentations." Not surprisingly, patriot-friendly publishers in New England had a different reaction. Outraged by the troops' alleged behavior, they shared the *Journal of Occurrences* with newspapers in other colonies, making it America's first news service.

By all accounts, the *Journal of Occurrences* had the desired effect. But this correspondence had more than an attitude. Journalism historians have grave doubts about the truthfulness of the accounts; they think Adams and company may have fabricated some or all of the reports to serve their own purposes.

And these journalistic sins of commission (by our standards today) were matched by equally significant sins of omission. There's little indication, for example, that either side printed fair and balanced coverage of events that might have influenced the attitudes people formed in the run-up to war. Readers likely heard little about British political figures, including Edmund Burke, who pleaded with Parliament and the King to find a nonmilitary solution to the growing polarization of attitudes on both sides of the Atlantic to preserve business and political relations with the colonists. Perhaps, as American children are taught in school, the King's intransigence made war inevitable, but I can't help wondering how things might have turned out if the masses on both sides of the ocean had been exposed to the whole truth by a vigorous press, rather than being manipulated by what amounted to propaganda from opposing camps vying for their allegiance.

After the war, freedom of the press remained, as A. J. Liebling so sagely observed, in the hands of those who owned the presses. Technological advances allowed newspaper publishers to increase production and lower their prices, which put the paper into the hands of more readers than ever. The newspaper became an especially important source of information for common, working folks, many of them immigrants, who trusted journalists to tell them what they needed and wanted to know as they sought a new life in a new land.

In the great circulation races of the nineteenth century, the news industry violated readers' trust repeatedly. Neither reporters nor publishers subscribed to anything like a code of ethics. That freed them to print whatever would attract the public and sell papers. Newspaper content expanded beyond business news and partisan political reporting to more sensationalistic fare such as crime stories and social scandals. Some stories, entirely fabricated, were simply meant to entertain. A classic example, from the New York Sun in 1835, was a serialized account of the discovery of life on the moon, complete with illustrations showing readers what moon people looked like. Much as Orson Welles's listeners had assumed that an alien invasion was really underway because they heard it on the radio, many nineteenth-century newspaper readers believed if the "life on the moon" story was in the paper, it must be true.

Perhaps the most outrageous and dangerous violation of readers' faith grew out of the profit-driven circulation battle between Joseph Pulitzer and William Randolph Hearst. From their powerful perch as the owners of the most widely read newspapers in the country, the two men indulged their press freedom to publish false stories that agitated the public and forced a reluctant President to commit U.S. troops to a war against Spain. Historians have labeled this fabricated, sensationalized news Yellow Journalism. These journalists were so far from any concern about telling the truth that Hearst could cable a newspaper illustrator who wanted to return home from Cuba because the troops he'd been sent to draw weren't fighting: "You provide the pictures, and I'll provide the war."

> Much as Orson Welles's listeners had assumed that an alien invasion was really underway because they heard it on the radio, many nineteenth-century newspaper readers believed if the "life on the moon" story was in the paper, it must be true.

Ironically, a real commitment to truth-telling rose out of this century of journalistic excess and infidelity. And, no matter what you think of its content and editorial stance today, the change was driven largely by the *New York Times.* The *Times* was a struggling daily paper when Adolph Ochs bought it in 1896. Ochs wanted to compete with other New York papers for readers, but he chose not to pander to the partisan, sensationalistic tastes indulged by Hearst and Pulitzer. He instructed his reporters and editors to cover the news, political and otherwise, in a fair and balanced way. The *New York Times* would strive for objectivity. The word "objectivity" had already begun circulating in news circles, but many historians credit Ochs with being the first to make it the ideological platform of his paper.

Ochs may not have taken the journalistic high road for entirely unselfish reasons. Some historians suggest that he chose objectivity as a strategy for competing in the circulation wars after reasoning that nonpartisan reporting would attract both

Democrats and Republicans, thus boosting readership. Other observers think Ochs had both readers and advertisers in mind. Reporting that split matters down the middle would be less likely to offend the sensibilities of the public or the advertisers who wanted to sell them products. Balanced news was just good business sense. If that was Ochs's primary concern, it worked extremely well. Advertising revenue soon outstripped subscriptions and street sales as the newspaper's largest source of income. Even the sensationalistic publishers like Hearst and Pulitzer began hiring reporters who could write stories based on facts.

To be fair, we must recognize that objective journalism did more than boost the bottom line. It also served society by nudging news and its practitioners away from the sideshow carnival atmosphere (and the sleight-of-hand journalism that implied) toward truth-telling, and it attracted reporters, many of them from middle- or working-class backgrounds, willing to seek the truth wherever it could be found, and report it to the public. These people established the hard-nosed journalistic traditions Laurie Garrett described in her good-bye memo to colleagues at *Newsday*. In its most dedicated form, this sort of reporting produced what we know today as investigative journalism. Ida Tarbell exposed the corrupt business practices of Standard Oil. Nelly Bly (born Elizabeth Cochran) threw open the door on American sweatshops. Journalists exposed the tragedy of child labor and the horror of insane asylums. For some historians of journalism, the period around the turn of the twentieth century marks the high point of American reporting.

Public enthusiasm for this sort of truth-telling eventually waned, a surprising development given our basic drive for information. How can we explain it? Some historians blame it on Teddy Roosevelt, the popular President who initially supported investigative journalism, but later labeled it muckraking, when it focused on indiscretions committed by his political and industrial allies. Roosevelt's allusion to John Bunyan's character in *Pilgrim's Progress*, who spends his days looking down and digging through the muck rather than looking up toward the goodness of God and humanity, helped paint a negative and inaccurate picture of these crusading reporters that persists today.

Perhaps the public simply grew tired of dealing with an endless stream of revelations about business and political wrongdoing that carried with them the implicit obligation to do something about them. Whatever the reasons, it would be more than a half century before investigative journalism attracted the attention of the press and the public to the same degree. But all was not lost in the interim; the experiences around the turn of the twentieth century left the expectation of objective journalism, or at least an approximation of it, embedded in American newsrooms and in the minds of the American public.

Soon after the decline of investigative journalism, two new forms of technology arose, with the potential to compete with newspapers and magazines in telling the truth—radio and television. Reaction to the *War of the Worlds* broadcast demonstrates clearly how much the public embraced and believed in radio as a source of information. When television arrived thirty years later, people turned to it in such numbers that churches, the original source of truth in society, cancelled some of their services; the pews were empty; everyone was at home in front of the TV.

With people paying that much attention, did radio and television station owners deliver the goods? The first content on the first commercial radio station—KDKA in Pittsburgh—sounded promising; it was returns from the 1920 Presidential election. But the bulk of radio programming, the stuff that attracted audiences and made radio a financially satisfying investment for owners and advertisers, was entertainment: comedies, drama, quiz shows, and music. When the federal government required stations to provide some news and information, most stations met that obligation by reading stories from the newspaper, at least until publishers objected. After a time, radio networks and stations hired news staffs, often former newspaper reporters, but they tended to rely on the same wire services newspapers used for much of their content. In the minds of owners, radio news might help burnish the image of the company, but it wasn't likely to make much direct contribution to the bottom line, therefore, why spend a lot of money on it?

Television followed a nearly identical course. It copied its content almost directly from radio—comedy, drama, quiz shows—and dedicated little of its broadcast day, in the beginning, to news. As with radio, TV network and station owners invested in news programming, which the government required, more for public relations purposes than financial benefit.

Can we identify, in the history of radio and television news, the same commitment to objective, trustworthy journalism—to telling the truth—that developed in the print world? My friends on the print side of the aisle would be inclined to answer, "No." Broadcast news, they have often told me, is superficial and derivative; any truth it manages to convey is probably copied from some print source. If you want to know what stories will be on the *CBS Evening News* Monday night, read the Sunday *New York Times*. Broadcasters, my print friends would say, are performers first and journalists only secondarily, if at all.

Even the dean of American news broadcasters, Edward R. Murrow, expressed doubts about the value of the contribution his chosen profession made to society. In a 1958 speech to the Radio-Television News Directors Association in Chicago he said, "One of the basic troubles with radio and television news is that both instruments have grown up as an incompatible combination of show business, advertising and news. Each of the three is a rather bizarre and demanding profession. And when you get all three under one roof, the dust never settles." Note that Murrow listed news as the last ingredient added to the radio stew. Yet there are instances of both forms of electronic media and the news people who staff them rising to something close to their potential as truth-tellers.

For radio, that moment came as the United States was

dragged into the tragic violence of World War Two. No event generates a greater need to know than a war, especially when a society's fathers and mothers, sons and daughters ship out to fight in it. Worried families learned what was happening from the newspaper, but radio and its live reports gave them a sense of what it was like for their loved ones in a dangerous place. This wasn't a make-believe alien invasion; it was the real sounds from the rooftops of London as the German air force tried to bomb the British into submission. It was the words of professional journalists, Ed Murrow among them, translating what they saw and heard across the battlefields of Europe into truth the folks at home desperately wanted to know. The broadcasts helped unify the nation and strengthened the American people's connection to their loved ones and their allies across the sea.

If you believe the hype that surrounds television news today, you might be tempted to think it has been a nonstop source of truth since it began in the 1950s. We know that's not true, but television has had some powerful moments. One of them came on February 27, 1968, after the most trusted man in America, Walter Cronkite, paid a visit to Vietnam to assess the progress of the American war against communism. A veteran of battlefield reporting and supporter of the U.S. war effort in Southeast Asia, Cronkite returned home and told the CBS News audience that what he saw in Vietnam convinced him the war was unwinnable. Was Cronkite telling the truth? Reaction from the Johnson administration suggests he was. The President issued no statements branding Cronkite an unpatriotic liar. In fact, legend has it that he turned to aides after the broadcast and told them losing Cronkite's support meant losing public support for the war, as well.

Television news broadcast what may have been its finest moment fourteen years earlier, when CBS News and Ed Murrow took on the powerful anti-communist Senator Joseph McCarthy. These were frightening times. The godless Communist Joseph Stalin (an uneasy ally, at best, during World War Two) had launched aggressive forays beyond Russia's borders to form the Soviet Union. American leaders made the American people aware of their fear that if unopposed the tentacles of Communism would stretch out until they threatened the very bastion of Christian democracy—the United States. The face-off between Soviet expansionism and American determination to resist it played out in the 50s and 60s arms race we know today as the Cold War, a war fought with the specter of nuclear bomb mushroom clouds that the people of the earth still live under today.

In Washington, in the early 1950s, Senator Joseph McCarthy made a play for power and influence by fanning American fear of communism into a full-blown Red Scare. By 1954, McCarthy had managed to use well timed but largely unsubstantiated allegations of Communist infiltration and sympathizing to set off a nationwide witch hunt that destroyed the reputations and careers of dozens of innocent people. Ed Murrow, newly assigned to TV after his distinguished radio news service in wartime, and his producer, Fred Friendly, decided that the senator had to be stopped. They did it by dedicating an entire edition of the program "See It Now" to exposing McCarthy. In a brilliant journalistic move, they let McCarthy tell the truth about himself by showing the audience film clips of the Senator viciously attacking the political attitudes and affiliations of ordinary people. Viewers' repulsion over McCarthy's mad dog tactics overrode their worries about Communism. Public opinion shifted dramatically, and the Senator's reign of terror soon ended.

## So What?

From this admittedly cursory review of journalism history, can we confirm or deny nostalgic memories of a time, not so long ago, when tough-minded, blue-collar types staffed the newsrooms of America, bound and determined to tell the truth as they understood it and let the chips fall where they may? We know many reporters came to embrace the idea of objective reporting (especially in the twentieth century) and, as long as it put money in the till, owners encouraged it. So, yes, we can confirm the memories, but we must beware of deifying anyone along the path of journalistic history.

In their commitment to sorting out the truth, reporters and publishers remain ordinary human beings subject to the influence of their own attitudes and public opinion. That might explain why the mainstream press took so long to provide fair and balanced coverage of the anti-slavery movement before the Civil War, and, for many years, paid little attention to often violent racism and the civil rights movement that existed side-by-side after the war. Selective perception might help us understand how Ida Tarbell could dedicate years of her life to documenting the facts about Standard Oil, but withhold her considerable talents from the suffragist movement struggling to tell the truth at the same time. Tarbell's traditional attitudes about the role of women may have prevented her from perceiving the justice of the women's cause. But we can't blame the truth-telling shortcomings of the news entirely on reporters' prejudices. Ironically, some of the fault lies in the practices or routines news people developed on their way to fair and balanced news. We'll take a closer look at news professionals and the way they do their jobs in chapter five.

> In their commitment to sorting out the truth, reporters and publishers remain ordinary human beings subject to the influence of their own attitudes and public opinion.

*Chapter Five*

# The Public Challenge: Routines of Truth-Telling

> The lowest form of popular culture—
> lack of information, misinformation,
> and a contempt for the truth or the reality
> of most people's lives—has overrun real
> journalism. Today, ordinary Americans
> are being stuffed with garbage.
>
> • Carl Bernstein

### Getting the Job Done

Objectivity is a great example of news practices influencing the truth news media tell. In theory, objectivity means reporters will attempt to communicate the information they collect in a fair and accurate way, devoid of their personal opinions. In practice, it opens the door for unscrupulous people to foist lies on the public. Joe McCarthy, the Red Baiting demagogue brought down, in part, by television news, relied on objective journalists (and their respect for the word of a Senator) to transmit his unsubstantiated allegations of Communist sympathizing word-for-word to their readers and listeners. To prevent reporters from verifying his charges he often released them just before their deadlines, which meant McCarthy's lies made it into the paper and the minds of readers and listeners unchallenged. Had reporters held McCarthy's "facts" until they could check them or give his targets a chance to respond, the Senator's power might never have grown so great and the careers of a great many Americans, especially in media industries, might have been saved untold amounts of pain and suffering.

Some journalists believe that even a balanced presentation of arguments on both sides of an issue falls short of the truth. They decry what they call a simple-minded objectivity, which gives the impression that the conflict at the heart of the story has only two sides and the arguments on both sides have equal merit. It may be, they say, that there are actually several sides to the issue, a whole raft of arguments, and some of those arguments are more convincing than others. According to this school of thought, the reporter has an obligation to weigh all of the arguments and facts she can gather, and give readers or listeners her fair and honest assessment of the situation. Truth becomes a far more complex beast in this case.

> Some journalists believe that even a balanced presentation of arguments on both sides of an issue falls short of the truth.

News directors and editors crave conflict; it may be *the* most basic criterion for determining if an event or an issue is news. But the news business, especially on the broadcast side, avoids complexity like the plague. (News consultants don't think it plays well on TV.) That aversion effectively rescues reporters from the Solomonic task of weighing and presenting multiple arguments. They're forced to boil it down to as few sides as possible, preferably two, and get in the paper or on the air. That reduction process means that even the most conscientiously compiled news account by the world's most objective reporter is likely to be missing some of the truth by the time we sit down to read or watch it.

## Deadlines

Time is the enemy of any reporter committed to telling the truth. Almost every assignment comes with a deadline attached. The word "deadline" originally referred to a part of a machine that did not move. In the news business, it means the day or time when a journalist must turn in his report. The mechanics of printing or broadcasting the news tend to make deadlines as rigid as an inflexible machine part. Editors and producers need time to lay out a newspaper and assemble audio and video for radio and TV, which means the reporter has to finish her job and turn in the story well before press or air time. If they stay on the job long enough, reporters learn to live with the stress inflicted by deadlines, but some never reconcile themselves to the limits deadlines impose on their efforts to discover the truth about the issue they're assigned to cover. Regardless of their internal conflict over getting the job done and doing the job right, the shortcuts they are forced to take to get a story in on time (such as only talking to one source, leaving out important sound bites or facts, or neglecting to confirm allegations leveled by a public official) can shortchange those of us who want to know the whole truth about a situation. It was deadline pressure more than anything else that allowed Joe McCarthy to spread his anti-communist lies. Savvy politicians still take advantage of it to get false or misleading ideas into print or on the air.

## The News Hole

Time (in broadcast news) and space (its equivalent in print news) conspire against thoroughness in reporting. In radio and television, news managers long ago decided that long stories drive people away, and that damages audience size estimates or ratings. The success of *USA Today* suggests that the same philosophy works in print, too. The bigger the audience, the higher the advertising rates, and the more money owners make on the operation. The shorter the story, the less information it contains. Once again, commerce triumphs over the quest for truth. Charges that broadcast news is superficial, little more than newspaper headlines, have been lobbed at the business for decades. Critics have labeled papers like *USA Today* the fast

food version of print news. But as long as news managers believe shorter stories generate and hold bigger audiences, that's
what we'll get.

In print (and broadcast), the space available for stories is
known as the *news hole*. Obviously, the larger the news hole
the greater the potential for telling the truth. In post-colonial
America, around the time that publishers and advertisers discovered they could be mutually beneficial to each other, the
news filled about seventy-five percent of the paper; ads took up
the other twenty-five percent. Today, the split is roughly sixty/
forty with sixty percent reserved for advertising. Print news re-
tains the potential to provide readers with more information
than broadcast, but with advertising's share of the space growing, we have to question the owners' commitment to doing so.

## We're Live

Time and technology have conspired in broadcast news to
complicate the conscientious journalist's life and our efforts to
understand the truth. Broadcasters can now report the news
live, as it happens. What better way could there be to serve our
natural need to know? Networks and stations bank on our surveillance drive as they trumpet their live exploits to attract audience. The attraction of live reporting has led networks and local
stations to serious abuses of the already limited time available
for telling the truth. The basic mechanics of a live shot require
an introduction for the anchors to read, followed by some sort
of introduction from the reporter, and then some sort of inter-
action between the news desk and the correspondent after he
or she has delivered whatever facts are available. All of those in-
troductory and closing comments sap time from the news hole
and reduce the amount of truth the reporter can provide.

Local stations often send reporters back to the scene of an
event or public meeting and have them report live to jazz up the
newscast. In those instances, the reporter is reduced to gesturing

to an empty room or a darkened building and informing us that there were live human beings in the area some time ago. The newscast producer has given us a "live report," but the reporter might have been able to provide us with more information if she had been given the time it took to get into and out of a live shot to write and assemble a well-organized, packaged report.

> The attraction of live reporting has led networks and local stations to serious abuses of the already limited time available for telling the truth.

Live broadcasts can serve a greater good. Warning a community to avoid a toxic chemical spill can save lives. Few broadcast moments did more to unify the American people in tremulous times than live coverage of President John F. Kennedy's funeral in 1963. On the other hand, live coverage of O. J. Simpson driving down a California freeway after his ex-wife was murdered provided little information ordinary people could use in making meaning of the world.

But sensationalistic content is not the most serious threat live news reporting poses to truth-telling. At its worst, the ability to go live dangerously short-circuits the reporting process. The time it takes an engineer to fire up the live truck is far shorter than the time a reporter needs to do the job right. Reporters often find themselves in front of a live camera before they've had time to collect and verify the facts of a situation. The information they deliver to the audience may be inaccurate or flat-out wrong. When the issue involved is a minor one, the worst result might be a slightly embarrassed journalist. In more drastic times, a rush to reporting might well traumatize millions of people. That was certainly the case in 1981, when ABC News mistakenly informed the nation that Ronald Reagan's press secretary James Brady had been killed in an assassination attempt on the President, when he had actually been wounded.

More recently, in 2005, instant reporting on the Hurricane

Katrina disaster that devastated parts of the Gulf Coast tragically misled the American public and may well have prolonged
the suffering of the storm's victims. Television reporters jumped
in front of live cameras shortly after the storm reached land to
inform the nation of widespread looting and violence in flood-
ravaged areas of New Orleans. Only later did we learn that the
reporters had it very wrong. Careful reporting, mostly by print
journalists, failed to confirm the vast majority of allegations
flashed to the world by TV news. There's no way to measure,
after the fact, what impact such reports had on the public's
willingness to come to the aid of the storm's victims. Live TV
news also dutifully allowed the Bush administration to delay
public awareness of how inadequate federal response had been.
Soon after Katrina hit, reporters went live to tell viewers FEMA
Director Michael Brown was surprised how big the hurricane
turned out to be. Had they bothered to check, those reporters
would have known the feds were given more than fair warning
to expect the worst. Again, Americans and the rest of the world
only learned the truth later, after lives had been lost and international opinion of the United States and its ability to care for
its own had been severely tarnished.

## Choosing the News

Before a reporter begins gathering information for a story, someone has to decide that it *is* a story. Editors and news directors generally make that call, relying on input from reporters
and on a commonly accepted set of criteria for what's news.
As we've already noted, conflict (preferably of the two-sided
kind) ranks *number one* for most journalists. The rest of the list
often includes timeliness (when did it happen?), significance
(how many people are effected by what happened?), proximity
(where did it happen?), human interest (does what happened
touch an ordinary person's emotions?), the unusual (how common is this event?), and uniqueness (has anything like this ever

happened before?). These are the qualities that attract news managers whose training and experience have taught them that if they find stories based on these criteria interesting, so will their audiences. Few stories contain every one of these elements, but if editors and news directors don't perceive some of them in a story idea, they won't assign a reporter to work on it. In that sense, news managers have total control over which truth and how much of it reporters can tell us.

This organizational structure can be leave hard-working journalists frustrated and the public ill-informed about critical events in the world. Historians cite American reporting on the Holocaust as an extreme example of the news system failing the people. U.S. journalists in Germany warned their editors that Hitler posed a dangerous threat to the Jews from the moment the Nazis ascended to power in 1933. But their editors, for a number of reasons including assurances to the contrary from American and German diplomats, discounted the concern. When reporters began filing reports of Nazi atrocities, the editors either failed to publish them or buried them somewhere deep in the paper, signaling to the public they didn't think the developments were very significant. As the Holocaust spread so did the war, and American editors turned their attention to U.S. military activity in Europe, again assigning less importance to what was happening in Nazi concentration camps. A few publishers eventually editorialized about the problem, joining the public's call for American leaders to help rescue the Jews, but by then most of the killing was over.

Fifty years later, American news values continue to relegate tragic stories of human suffering elsewhere in the world to less prominent positions in the paper or their newscasts, if they bother to mention them at all. In one hundred days in 1994, Hutu militias in Rwanda slaughtered an estimated one million people—Tutsis and politically moderate Hutus—with little notice by Western journalists. Critics point out that reporters who did file stories on refugees fleeing the killing fields usually failed to understand what was happening, and the tone of their coverage tended to suggest that it was some sort of ethnic thing between wild, African tribes. Most detailed journalistic clarification came after the fact, after innocent men, women, and children had been hacked to death with machetes.

And the preoccupation with matters closer to home (or perhaps it's simply negligence on the part of American news media) continues. As of January 2006, fighting between rebels and government forces raged in the Darfur region of western Sudan. Many considered it genocide, with a death toll since the shooting began in 2003 estimated at more than 400,000. American news media ran some stories about Darfur, but human rights observers pointed out that most of their accounts continued to downplay the magnitude of the killing by relying on an estimated death toll of 70,000 produced by the United Nations two years earlier.

Many of today's news managers, under immense pressure to boost audience and their company's bank account, tend to favor stories that meet news criteria from the bottom of the list—human interest, the unusual, the unique. They pander more to our common curiosity than our deeper desire to understand the world around us. And in the space or time that could have been used to explore significant issues, we get what some people call *infotainment*.

Infotainment crept into my newsroom as it has most news organizations by now. Its presence became most obvious during "sweeps weeks"; the four months of the year when Nielsen estimated the size of our audience. Stations use those estimates to set advertising rates. To boost the numbers, we always produced "special reports" to attract more viewers. In earlier days, management readily approved topics with significant social value. But in later years, the standards obviously changed. For example, I repeatedly offered to do a special series on the rapid influx of Latinos, attracted by the prospect of good manufacturing jobs, into our area. One town's population had gone from virtually all Anglo to twenty percent Hispanic in barely a decade. The transition was not without some friction. I thought it was important to talk to people from both cultures and provide our viewers with information that might promote better understanding. My news director rejected the idea every time, usually without explaining why it didn't measure up. In its place, we ran reports on what it took to re-do a backyard or talked our way into places the public normally wasn't allowed to go, stories our consultant told us would grab viewers.

## Just Doing the Job

More and more in today's commercial news environment, owners expect journalists to entertain readers and viewers; it's considered part of the job. And the bright, talented people who enter the news business are fully capable of doing it. In fact, in the last years of my career, it seemed to me that the young people entering the business preferred lighter fare. They had the training needed for serious reporting; they demonstrated that in the newsroom. If someone called with a tip on a hot political or business story, they sat down and took careful notes. But when they hung up, they didn't race to the news director and plead for time to dig up the rest of the details. Often, they ambled over and dropped the notes on the desk of an older reporter, smiled, and suggested he might be interested in what the caller had to say. Sometimes these fresh young journalists stated flat out that they wanted to do feature stories. That must have been music to the ears of the new generation of managers, people who often land their positions through the efforts of station consultants who constantly bombard them with story ideas (read: infotainment) that have proven to boost ratings in other markets. It doesn't take too much thinking to realize that the more time and space dedicated to entertaining the audience, the less time and space available for information about issues and events that touch our lives deeper than our taste buds, our hair color, or the grass in our backyard.

Watching young journalists surrender so readily to the gods of infotainment was disappointing, but it doesn't mean there are no serious reporters left. When asked to describe their role as a journalist, most news workers don't celebrate the superficial side of their job. They tend to see themselves performing a combination of significant functions including objective transmission of information, analysis or interpretation of that information, and surveillance of those in positions of power.

Each of these roles seems legitimate enough at first glance, but danger may lurk behind even what appears to be good intentions. We've already seen what simple-minded objectivity can lead to, in Senator Joseph McCarthy's infamous rise to power. To prevent unscrupulous people from bending the news to their own advantage, some reporters believe the job comes with an intrinsic need to examine the information they collect and, where necessary, provide the audience with some explanation of its significance. The question then becomes: What additional information will the reporter use to provide that analysis or context? Some observers would say that extra information comes directly from a reporter's own thoughts.

Critics, former journalists among them, have built a cottage industry out of leveling accusations that reporters tap their own attitudes and beliefs to flesh out a story, resulting in biased journalism. Usually, the charge is that reporting reflects the liberal bias of the journalist. The Project for Excellence in Journalism went looking for that bias by counting journalists' opinions (statements in a news story that are not attributed to any other source) in 2004 cable news coverage of the Iraq War. They found it. Two percent of CNN's war reports included the reporter or anchor's personal views. For MSNBC, the count worked out to twenty-nine percent. And Fox News, which over the years has drifted from the slogan "fair and balanced reporting" to "we report, you decide," included journalists' opinions in seventy-three percent of its war reports. The opinions on Fox

News generally favored the Bush administration. Watching Fox News might be a fairly comfortable experience, psychologically speaking, for those who share the network's views, but a steady diet of biased news, whatever ideological direction it tilts, denies us access to the whole truth about the issues and events that touch our lives. News workers committed to telling the truth and news consumers committed to learning the truth should not allow that to happen.

Journalists who embrace the third role mentioned above—watchdog of the powerful—stand a better chance of not falling into the bias trap. This role was already around in colonial days (John Peter Zenger was trying to hold the governor of New York accountable), but it blossomed with the advent of objective reporting and the rise of the muckraking era. Far from indulging their personal opinions, these reporters dug deep to find the truth. Ida Tarbell spent years researching Standard Oil so her charges against the abusive industrial giant would be based on fact. Reporters who accepted the watchdog role helped expose the Watergate Scandal and take down a corrupt President. This is the spirit of reporting Laurie Garrett applauded in her departure from *Newsday*, reporters who care if the governor lies or someone shuts off a poor man's heat in the middle of winter.

This type of reporting, of necessity, takes the reporter close to the rich and powerful, and therein lies a danger for the watchdog: a steady diet of up-close-and-personal exposure to the shortcomings of people can sour dedicated surveillance with cynicism. The journalist may still seek the truth, but past experience has taught her that even if you find it, the system has ways of resisting its effect when reporters place it in the hands of the public. Even a well-trained watchdog may be tempted to lie down on the job once in a while.

> Even a well-trained watchdog may be tempted to lie down on the job once in a while.

## Do You Know Who I Am?

Journalists are, as we have noted several times, only human, and that leaves them vulnerable to another side effect in addition to cynicism. The power to determine what information the public gets to read or hear can have a seductive influence. Over time, news workers may become overconfident of their judgment and develop an exaggerated sense of their own importance—in plain, simple language, they take off on an ego trip. It can happen on the local or the national level.

At the very least, self-important journalists simply may not be much fun to be around. A store clerk once shared with me the disgust she felt when a local reporter haughtily punctuated her displeasure with the service she was receiving in the store with the question, "Do you know who I am?" I remember the tone of voice Brit Hume (formerly of ABC News, now with Fox News) assumed at a Clinton campaign stop in 1996 as he imperiously informed my photographer and me (mere local TV news grunts) that the platform we had just scrambled onto was for *network* crews. Other than Hume's august presence, the platform was empty.

At its worst, journalistic arrogance can blind reporters, preventing them from seeing the truth we need to know. The 1988 Democratic National Convention in Atlanta is a case in point. Michael Dukakis was expected to receive the Presidential nomination, but he needed campaign support from fellow candidate Jesse Jackson and his Rainbow Coalition if he hoped to win. After the two camps met in Atlanta, NBC confidently reported that Jackson and his people had jumped behind Dukakis, a fact Jackson would confirm when he spoke that night. My crew had flown to Atlanta to monitor the Indiana delegation's involvement in the convention, and that included hanging out with the Indiana Black Caucus after Dukakis met with Jackson. It was clear from what we heard in that session that while Jackson's campaign was over, no one in the room planned to do much for Dukakis. At six o'clock, we told our viewers back in Indiana about the disparity between the network's conclusions and what we were hearing from black Democrats.

Jackson spoke at eight o'clock that night, but it wasn't the rip-roaring pep talk for Dukakis the network predicted. He closed with the rousing chant: "Keep hope alive! Keep hope alive! Keep hope alive!" The network correspondents interpreted that as a rallying cry for the now united campaigns. It struck us as code language to Jackson's Rainbow Coalition, urging them to keep the faith until his next campaign. In the end, Blacks never really got behind Dukakis, as the network said they'd agreed to. The national reporters got their information from powerful Democratic Party officials at the top of the news food chain, sources worthy of a network correspondent's attention. They didn't waste time listening to black delegates from good old Indiana. In the aftermath of the election, it seemed to me they might have done a better job of truth-telling if they had.

## According to Highly Placed Officials

Journalists gather story information a number of ways, including direct observation of a situation or event, reviewing documents, and conducting polls. But no source of information is more important than people. If no one ever announced anything, or if everyone refused to talk to reporters, they'd have very little to write or say. That simple fact of journalistic life creates a dependency on sources that can threaten the integrity of the news and impoverish our efforts to know the truth.

As the network correspondents did at the Democratic Convention in 1988, journalists tend to rely on the power holders in society as their primary source of information. If you want to know what the Democratic Party plans to do, you assume the party leaders are in the best position to make an official statement. If you need the details of a murder in the community, you assume the police chief (or a designated public information officer) is the best source of information. If the nation is at war, you expect the President or military leaders to provide updates on the action. Those assumptions have led many a reporter, including prestigious national correspondents, astray. In the best of all possible worlds, officials would speak honestly to reporters who could then pass the truth along to us. But little communication in our world is that objective and straightforward.

A lack of candor on the part of a source may explain how the network got it wrong in Atlanta in 1988. Forceful denials of the truth by highly placed German officials allowed them to hide the fact of the Holocaust from reporters during World War Two. Repeated lies about weapons of mass destruction, transmitted through news media, helped George W. Bush lead the United States into war with Iraq in 2003. Manipulation of the facts allowed a police chief in one of the cities I covered to announce a major reduction in the violent crime rate. Only after the public had been taken in by our reports did I learn the chief accomplished his miracle of crime prevention by shifting some serious offenses to other categories.

Reporters need to be wary of sources who trade on their relationship with news media to accomplish underhanded and sometimes sinister objectives. Politicians trying to gauge public reaction to an idea they're considering implementing commonly "leak" information to a select group of journalists on the condition that their name is not attached to it. For years, conscientious journalists resisted accepting information to which they couldn't tie a name (those "sources who would comment only if they weren't identified"). Some news organizations had a policy barring anonymous sources from their news reports. But protecting a source's identity has become a frequent practice in recent years, either because the "highly placed official" is offering information about a significant event or issue that news managers think the public should know or because they don't want to end up the only news organization in town that doesn't have it.

Sometimes sources demand anonymity because they fear reprisals for divulging the truth. Sometimes they seek to exact revenge against another public figure without having to answer for it in the court of public opinion. The outing of CIA operative Valerie Plame in 2003, apparently by a highly placed source in the White House because Plame's husband, a diplomat, publicly disagreed with the Bush administration, may be an example of the latter motive for pressuring reporters to withhold a source's name. Not knowing where information came from puts us at a disadvantage in our efforts to evaluate its truthfulness. There was some indication major American news organizations were moving away from the use of unnamed sources in 2005.

Why, you might be asking, would journalists allow themselves to be used this way? We know competition plays a role. And, in part, it's because they subscribe primarily to the journalistic role of disseminator; their job is to report what these officials say, whatever the conditions under which they agree to say it, as objectively as possible. But an equally important factor is their dependence on these sources. If a reporter writes a story questioning the accuracy or veracity of these official pronouncements or breaks a promise to protect an official's identity, she could lose the absolutely essential access to the sources themselves. You may think public or elected officials don't have the right to banish journalists from their presence or restrict their access to important information because they are offended by a story. But they do it. Fear of losing access or being thrown out discouraged some American reporters from filing stories critical of the Nazis as World War Two got underway. Residents of the White House have been known to restrict access for reporters they perceive to be their enemies. Mayors have been known to slam the door on local reporters. In one of the communities I covered, the sheriff's department stopped providing mug shots of criminal suspects because a reporter's story made their public information officer angry. Many a journalist has had to weigh the benefits of an exposé against the long-term loss of access to a source.

Journalists also depend on official sources because those individuals are, or should be, readily accessible, and that saves time for a reporter pressed up against the wall by a deadline. It also makes the job easier—why run around trying to pin down the facts yourself when one call to an official source can yield the answer you need? You run the risk of being misled, as McCarthy abused the reporters of his day, but what alternative do you have?

Actually, there may be lots of alternatives, other individuals in the country or the community who know a thing or two about the issue in question and could contribute to the completeness of a reporter's story. But I know, from twenty years in the news business, many of those voices have little or no chance of being heard. Why not? Because they're not *official*. Reporters tend to believe that in a free society, if you assume a position of public responsibility, you have an obligation to answer questions about what you do. Plus, journalists think a quote or a sound bite from an official source adds authority to their story. Quoting an ordinary citizen, no matter how well informed, doesn't carry the same clout. And, most unofficial sources haven't been vetted in any formal way. Reporters may not trust all official sources to the same extent, but they are inclined not to trust most unofficial sources at all. My colleagues and I often dismissed ordinary citizens who called to inform us about community problems as crackpots. Sometimes they were, but in the occasional instance when something the caller said had the ring of truth we actually checked it out. How? We called an official source, who usually assured us everything was alright. It's impossible to know how much truth we missed by following the official source routine.

Sources can threaten the truth-telling process in a more personal way. Often, the most important sources are also the most powerful, important people around. Reporters can fall under the spell of that power. Simply doing the job places journalists in close proximity to these movers and shakers. Politicians and captains of industry employ the "buddy" tactic at every level of our society. The savvy ones strike up a friendly relationship with the press, provide donuts and coffee at their news conferences, and encourage reporters to address them by their first name. Sometimes they invite select members of the press into their inner sanctum.

In one of his books, the late network anchor and correspondent David Brinkley recalls John F. Kennedy's late-night invitations for drinks at the White House. We don't know what effect those visits may have had on Brinkley's attitudes about and coverage of the President, but I know what effect socializing with the powerful had on one of my colleagues. When the former city controller was elected the new mayor of the city, this reporter, who drew the same paycheck as the rest of us for turning in fair, balanced, and objective reporting, stood up in the center of the newsroom and informed everyone that henceforth, if there were negative stories to tell about her friend the mayor, she would not be doing them. And she didn't. If all reporters pulled their punches to preserve their friendship with public figures, truth-telling in journalism would be a severely endangered species.

## All the News that Fits

Print journalists have long considered themselves superior to broadcast news media in terms of how thoroughly they can report the information they collect from sources. Every edition of the *New York Times* promises readers "all the news that's fit to print." Newspaper and newsmagazine reporters dismiss radio and television news, with their fifteen- or twenty-second stories, as little more than glorified headlines. And, after twenty years of wringing the less important facts out of the truth I gathered to make it fit an ever-shrinking time limit imposed by broadcast news managers, I am forced to admit there is truth to the charge. But in the modern era of corporate journalism, both broadcast and print reporters face challenges in how much truth they can deliver.

Ten years ago my colleagues on the print side of the aisle began murmuring about changes in the content of the newspaper that would reduce the mass of "news" publishers considered fit to print. Consultants had been brought in to advise the owners on what steps to take to increase circulation and remain competitive. These specialists, similar to the corps of advisors already grafted onto most broadcast news companies, generally did not recommend increasing the reporting staff or resurrecting the muckrakers. They talked about page design, layout, graphics, color photographs, and (right on cue) more features (read: infotainment). And where would those new features go? Often in the forty percent of the paper that had been dedicated to hard news, public issues, and important information reporters thought the public needed to know. The news staff might still be able to turn in objective stories on significant topics, but simple math tells us you can't subtract space from the news hole without reducing the amount of truth readers will find in it.

As the news hole shrank on the print side, it actually grew on the broadcast side. Owners discovered that they could attract as many listeners and viewers with news and information as they could with entertainment and at much less cost. More than an image builder, the news had become a moneymaker. Radio stations cashed in by replacing their music formats with news and talk. Television stations added more newscasts, morning, noon, and night. Network television, unable to convince affiliates to let them expand their evening newscasts, expanded their morning shows and created newsmagazines modeled on the very successful *60 Minutes* formula. Twenty-four-hour cable news channels sprang up. It all sounds like a truth-seeker's bonanza. But, when measured by the yardstick we've been using in this examination of news media, it falls far short.

## Is Talk the Truth?

We noted earlier that radio stations using the news/talk format were most likely to report increased revenue in 2004. They obviously delivered on their commercial obligation to their owners. The question we have to ask here is: How well did those stations deliver on their obligation to tell the truth to their listeners? Most news/talk radio stations provide brief, traditional newscasts throughout their broadcast day; these might qualify as factual accounts—the type of news we expect from professional journalists committed to objective reporting. But the bulk of the content on news/talk radio is talk, delivered by program hosts who make no promise to play by the accepted reporter's rules of the road. Despite that lack of commitment to objectivity, many of these "talkers" constantly assure their audience (millions of us listen every day) that they speak the truth about public issues and public figures. If they don't approach the issue in a fair and balanced way and don't engage in the standard verification process to determine the facts, as we would expect a journalist to do, how can they possibly arrive at the truth?

A closer look at the labels talk show hosts apply to themselves—conservative or liberal, mostly—may help us understand what these talkers are actually giving us. A standard dictionary definition of a conservative would be someone who likes things just the way they are, who is cautious and resists change. By contrast, a liberal is someone who favors liberty or reform, who is tolerant. Notice any similarities between the two definitions? They generally refer to *beliefs* people hold about the way things should be, to their general *attitudes* toward life. Talk show hosts form attitudes like any ordinary person, and we can expect them to filter any information they take in, about the physical world or the political sphere, through those attitudes, just as we are all inclined to do. That means that, no matter how they protest the possibility, their thoughts and conclusions are subject to the same selective processes as the rest of us.

Considering that they make no commitment to objectivity and fairness in their deliberations, it seems inevitable that much of what these hosts tell us on the radio (or in televised versions) is the result of unbridled selective exposure, perception, and memory—it's opinion, not fact. The "truth" they

Much of what these hosts tell us on the radio (or in televised versions) is the result of unbridled selective exposure, perception, and memory—it's opinion, not fact.

disseminate comes with a built-in bias, courtesy of the host's own attitudes. They may even tailor their remarks to suit our taste, pander to our prejudices, and ensure that listeners stay tuned in. (This is, after all, a business.)

A steady diet of talk radio strikes me as an unhealthy situation and a gigantic threat to our honest search for the truth. If our need to know is joined to a religiously based or humanitarian commitment to open-mindedness and fairness, we do ourselves a disservice by relying on talk shows of any stripe to tell us the truth. We know the truth can be elusive in the best of circumstances; in the talk show setting, it may elude us entirely.

## More News All the Time

And then there's television news, another paying proposition for owners. Local stations and networks have dramatically increased the amount of airtime dedicated to news and information programming. From a financial perspective, more newscasts mean more advertising revenue. But the increased news time should also bode well for truth-seekers, right? Wrong.

On the local level, adding new newscasts doesn't mean adding more reporting staff to gather even more news. In my experience, it meant repackaging the same information and spreading it out across the additional news time. Sometimes it meant covering less serious news than before because reporters were reassigned to infotainment fare. For instance, my station cancelled Saturday morning children's programming and replaced it with three hours of locally produced news. For a few minutes at the top of each hour we reported hard news, most of it recycled from the night before. The rest of the hour was filled with pet segments, restaurant reviews, vehicle test drives, live reports from charity toy collection sites or pregame tailgating activity in the parking lot of a local university, and, of course, frequent commercial breaks. We promoted every expansion of our news day as a service to the community. To those of us who wanted to make the best use of the available time to provide viewers with meaningful information, the new shows felt like angel food cake: attractive to look at, but not much to bite into. At least we didn't promote the shows as great sources of truth; that was good, because they weren't.

Expansion of network time for news and information has been equally disappointing, at least from a truth-seeker's point of view. CBS's long-running Sunday night hit, *60 Minutes*, taught national broadcasters that prime-time news programs could compete with entertainment fare and it was much less expensive to produce. That led to creation of shows like *Dateline*, *20/20*, *Prime Time Live*, and *48 Hours*, all of which began with a commitment to in-depth examination of serious issues and events. Then, the corporate bean counters and consultants stepped in. The pressure was on to build audience and reduce costs at the same time. The unfortunate solution was most obvious on *Dateline*. In place of thoughtful, carefully researched reports and investigations, we got irrelevance like hour-long versions of sensational trials (NBC made a deal with the Court TV cable channel) that touched little more than viewers' natural curiosity for the morbid and bizarre. And another promising avenue for truth-telling shut down. All of the major networks, broadcast and cable, have demonstrated the same ability to fritter away valuable news time with frivolous or sensationalistic fare. Pop star Michael Jackson's legal travails filled the screen for weeks, O. J. Simpson's murder trial seemed to last forever, and, in 2005, one network dedicated a full hour to a troubled young woman who ran off to avoid getting married. Networks have even fiddled with the content of their evening news programs, eliminating information that might help us understand our society and the world and filling the time they gain with stories that touch us only on a superficial level, if at all.

Have we been too harsh in assessing the volume of truth issuing from today's news media? It's hard to think so when you hear veteran reporters (like Laurie Garrett) expressing the same sentiments. Even Walter Cronkite, once voted the most trusted man in America, has chided his former colleagues for not reporting enough truth (In May, 2005, Cronkite told a United Nations panel that inadequate reporting had left Americans uninformed about our nation's obligations under international nuclear arms treaties). Before I left commercial television news, our viewers were complaining to me that they didn't get much out of our news anymore. Some of them told me they had turned to Public Broadcasting, where the stories are longer and the coverage is more global, for a more complete recounting of the truth. Most of these people did not consider themselves elitists, intellectuals, or even liberals; they were ordinary people with a natural need to know and understand. That desire for the truth was so great that they were willing to abandon their "friends" in commercial, mainstream news media to find it.

## The Power and the Money

As Ed Murrow so clearly explained in 1958, pressure to make money on the news, beginning in the post-Revolutionary War era, has always threatened the amount of truth reporters can deliver to the public. But the advent of objective journalism at least gave reporters a fighting chance. They used to talk about *the wall* that honest news organizations erected between the newsroom and the business office. The wall meant that owners could push the news department to generate stories that would attract readers and viewers. But the final decision on exactly which stories made it into the paper or on the air rested with news professionals, not the advertising or marketing departments. That is not the case at many news organizations today.

A notorious example appeared in the *Los Angeles Times* in the late 1990s. The paper put out a special edition of its Sunday magazine devoted to the city's new sports arena. What reporters and readers didn't know (before the issue came out) was that the *Times* had made a deal to share revenue from the special issue with the arena owners. When the news staff found out, they were furious about being used for such crassly commercial purposes. But assigning stories based on their attractiveness to business associates and advertisers poses a far more serious threat to a news organization's potential for telling the truth. As award-winning journalist James Risser put it in the January/February 2000 issue of the *Columbia Journalism Review*: "What's hard to measure is how many potentially tough and useful stories never get done, or are softened, because they might offend an advertiser. From there, it's only a small step to devoting time to stories and sections that actually will please the subjects and rake in ad money."

The wall protecting the newsroom from the fiddling fingers of the business side of the *Times* may have been nicked and scarred from occasional attacks over the years, but its days were numbered when a new CEO arrived (from an unrelated industry) and vowed to knock it down to boost the paper's bottom line. It was new management, intent on pleasing advertisers, that ended a longtime commitment to the wall at my local TV station in the Midwest, but they were more devious about it than the *Times* CEO. Our new manager promised the entire staff that we would engage in hard-hitting, advocacy journalism. But when those of us assigned to this new "consumer hotline" met with the boss to hear the ground rules of the operation, he informed us we would do "no retail." Why? Because that would put us on the trail of some of the station's most lucrative advertising accounts. In practice, it meant not being allowed to mention, let alone tell the truth about, routine overcharges by the service department at a local car dealership (a major advertiser). It meant being chastised by our chief executive for leaning on a local

lumberyard (another major advertiser) to clean up debris that
neighbors were tired of looking at. The truth was that the company had ignored complaints about the eyesore it had created
by dumping junk out the back door. But after an angry phone
call from the company to our general manager, the "truth" we
were ordered to tell our audience was that the clean up (actually
triggered by our investigation) was a voluntary, goodwill gesture
initiated by the lumberyard.

Evidence that the wall between the newsroom and the business side of news organizations is seriously eroded or perhaps
already lying in pieces on the ground can be found throughout
the news industry. The film *The Insider* chronicles the devastating impact corporate concerns about the effect even the threat
of lawsuits can have. CBS News producers had nailed down the
truth about malignant tobacco industry practices designed to
keep smokers hooked on cigarettes. But when a tobacco company started growling about taking the network to court if it
broadcast the information, the network caved in. Around the
same time that once-towering CBS News was cowering at the
feet of corporate America, ABC News was presenting tough-
minded reports, including one on Bosnian genocide in which
anchor and co-writer Peter Jennings would ask: "How did America's leaders decide to stand by for so long while scenes of mass
murder and genocide were once again enacted on European
soil?" But when another tobacco giant took offense over ABC's
reporting, the network backed down and paid up big time.

A young producer at a local TV station in upstate New York
told me the topics his investigative team chose to tell the truth
about had to satisfy managers that they would attract the right
audience and boost ratings. Much like the *Los Angeles Times*,
local newspapers and broadcasters plan special sections and
segments that will generate revenue for the news operation and
the advertisers who sponsor the coverage. A local TV station in
one of the communities where I worked systematically offered
extended coverage of individual towns and cities in its viewing

area. It's significant, I think, that the station sales staff descended on the town before the reporters arrived.

We have to ask how much straight-from-the-shoulder, bare-knuckled truth will be delivered in journalism spawned by the marketing department. The finished product may look like news; reporters apply the same basic skills in gathering it. But we need to be cautious about accepting the information as the whole truth; it's likely the rough edges and downsides have been deleted to satisfy all the business interests involved. And, as James Risser suggested, we have to ask what important stories could have been covered, what truth told, in the space occupied by these thinly veiled promotional efforts?

Commercialism may not be the only corrosive force breaking down the wall and limiting the truth reporters bring to us. Some critics see more insidious forces at work. They accuse the wealthy and powerful of conspiring to manipulate media messages to maintain their dominance over society. These critics tend to see human life as a class struggle, with the rich and powerful elite pitted against the interests of the masses. This elite class formulated the Magic Bullet Theory in the early days of mass media. Publicly, they said that common people were ill equipped to cope with the messages delivered by print and broadcast. In their hearts, they believed the media were capable of communicating too much truth to the masses, truth that ordinary people might be tempted to act on and overthrow the traditional balance of power.

The fears of the elite are not entirely misplaced. You may recall that patriot leaders of the Revolutionary War enlisted the masses in the revolutionary cause by using print media to sell them on ideas like independence and the natural rights of life, liberty, and the pursuit of happiness. It worked; common people signed up to fight. But after the war, when American merchants had broken free of British economic oppression, they hoped common people would return to their "normal" place at the bottom of society. The people, sold on the freedoms promised them in a democracy, occasionally exercised their rights by reacting to actions by business and political leaders that they considered discriminatory and oppressive, often with tragic results. Some of the saddest stories in American history are tales of laborers standing up to unjust and inhumane employers, only to be beaten down by soldiers in the service of the nation those workers' ancestors fought to create.

Although the masses always lost, the upheaval left the upper classes uneasy and on the lookout for influences that could stir up the working class again. The advent of modern print and broadcast media made them wary, indeed. The Magic Bullet Theory was one of their responses. If nothing else, it frightened ordinary people enough to convince them to put limits on how much mass media—books, newspapers, films, radio, television, and even comic books—their children were exposed to. As we've already noted, many people still believe the Magic Bullet Theory today (even though it was seriously discredited by scientific research) and shield their children from media messages and whatever truth they might contain.

Another elite response, according to some critics, is making sure they can control the content of popular mass media and eliminate or challenge messages that might diminish their wealth and power. The simplest method is to own the media, and exercise total control over the information—the truth—the masses receive. That's certainly what Hearst and Pulitzer did in the days of Yellow Journalism. Today's trend toward consolidation of news organizations under fewer and fewer corporate logos sets up the same scenario. Of course, companies buying up newspapers and electronic media insist their only motivation is profit. But bear in mind that when Rupert Murdoch, head of the massive News Corporation, was asked if holding a near-monopoly on the news tempted him to impose his own ideology on his news organizations, his answer was, "Yes." At the very least, corporate ownership and the centralization of decision making that goes with it reduce the number of minds trying to understand the truth of our world and diminish the number of distinct voices the public can seek out in trying to establish the reality of an issue or event.

Short of exercising total control, critics suggest, the elite conspire from their positions of privilege and power to influence what the public is told. Despite my mother's insistence that in America even a middle-class kid like me could hope to be President someday, the levers of power in this country, much like freedom of the press, are most available to those who can afford to purchase them. The money to play in politics, with some exceptions, comes from the business world, a fact of life that has long since forged a tremendous bond between industry and government. No less a luminary than President Dwight D. Eisenhower warned us of the danger of too close a connection between the private sector and the public sphere (particularly the military) in his 1961 farewell speech to the nation. "In the councils of government," he said, "we must guard against the acquisition of unwarranted influence. . . . The potential for the disastrous rise of misplaced power exists and will persist. We must never let the weight of this combination endanger our liberties or democratic processes. . . . Only an alert and knowledgeable citizenry can compel the proper meshing of the huge industrial and military machinery of defense with our peaceful methods and goals, so that security and liberty may prosper together."

Critics would argue that Eisenhower's perceptive words have gone unheeded. Rather than contributing to an "alert and knowledgeable" society, news media have been complicit, intentionally and unintentionally, in limiting how much the public knows about what's being done in our name, at home and abroad. By disseminating only what they're told and relying overwhelmingly on official (government) sources, news media have unintentionally deprived us of the whole truth about a host of actions taken by our government. Some critics accuse news organizations of being in league with the powers that be, intentionally reporting only the official point of view in a conspiracy to maintain the status quo, that is, to keep society's wealth and power where it has always been.

Suspicion of news media extends all the way down to the basic decision-making process. Why, some critics ask, do newspapers and broadcast news organizations regularly cover mergers and acquisitions and devote pages and pages to stock market activity, but only pay attention to workers when they protest owners' policies with walkouts, picketing, and strikes? Why do newspapers and broadcasters run "stories" announcing the opening of a new big box department store, but pay little attention to the painfully small wages and benefits those giant corporations provide to their employees?

Critics blame this neglect of important information—this failure to provide fair and balanced news—on reporters (many of whom, they say, come from privileged backgrounds), but they hold owners, who belong to the elite they serve, principally responsible for delivering less than the whole truth. The long-term effect on news consumers, according to some researchers, is that they begin to accept this manipulated version of the truth as reality, and stop looking for truth anywhere else. Karl Marx may have believed that religion served as "the opiate of the people" in his day. But today, critics would say, mass media have taken over that function. By convincing a credulous public that news media deliver all the news that's worth knowing, and then telling them only what the elite want them to know, news organizations help maintain the balance of wealth and power in society.

This explanation for the shape and content of the news we receive only works if two things are true: reporters are willing to ignore their commitment to objective journalism and people are really as incapable of analyzing the information they receive as the Magic Bullet Theory (and society's elite) want to believe. As both a journalist and an ordinary citizen, I am reluctant to accept either of those assumptions. But, other than crass pandering to profit-making, I don't have a better theory to explain

why mainstream news media, at all levels, pay so much attention to the issues important to the elite and have so little interest in the problems facing the lower class and minorities in
America. As it was from the beginning, and is now more than
ever, news is first and foremost a business. If tailoring the news
to the interests of the elite and ignoring the struggles of the less
fortunate produces the desired profit margin, that's likely to be
the path news company owners will follow.

Critics also argue that any news organization that breaks the
rules and puts out a story that questions the official line will be
whipped back into shape. These tactics take several forms. One
is financial. Political leaders can instruct bureaucrats to make
life more difficult for a company that reports the wrong news.
For instance, a corporation looking to acquire more media
outlets can find itself facing antitrust questions. In 2004 and
2005, the Federal Communications Commission began leveling
massive fines against broadcasters whose content was deemed
"indecent." Fear of economic reprisals led one broadcast organization to drastically censor the language in the film *Saving
Private Ryan*, one of the most realistic portrayals of the truth
of war ever produced. Worries that President George W. Bush's
anger over a report criticizing his military service might lead to
heavy fines and business complications may explain why CBS
News anchor Dan Rather stepped down earlier than he planned
to, and why the head of CBS's parent company (Viacom) made a
virtually unprecedented public appearance to deny any political
motivation behind the story.

Even Public Broadcasting, an entity created largely with
government funding, charged with providing listeners and
viewers with a diversity of voices and ideas, is not immune.
The Corporation for Public Broadcasting, which doles out a
congressionally-approved allowance to the Public Broadcasting
System, National Public Radio, and local stations, has launched
a crusade to reverse what officials labeled public broadcasting's
unacceptable tilt to the liberal or left-wing side of the issues.

The witch hunt is accompanied by threats to cut off funding. Government appropriations for noncommercial broadcasting have been declining for twenty years; withholding funds from content that doesn't pass inspection would effectively starve some programs to death. Citing a multitude of conservatively oriented programs already airing on public stations, some observers accuse political leaders of trying to stamp out any vestige of balance in public broadcasting. If that's true, it spells bad news for listeners and viewers, like my Midwestern friends, who recognized the shortcomings of commercial news media and gravitated to NPR and PBS in search of more complete truth about the issues of the day.

Another common tactic critics accuse the elite of employing is *flak*. Flak entered the American lexicon during World War Two; it was anti-aircraft fire (originally from a German gun called the Flak) sent aloft to disable or scare off enemy warplanes. Used figuratively in the news context, it might mean a phone call from a high-ranking government official directly to a newspaper publisher or a network president, reprimanding them for the "shabby" work done by their employees or even threatening some sort of retaliation if the offending information isn't qualified or withdrawn.

One of the most colorful bits of flak was sent up by Attorney General John Mitchell during the Watergate Scandal, when he reportedly told *Washington Post* reporter Carl Bernstein: "All that crap, it's all been denied. If you print that, Katie Graham [the publisher of the *Post* who stood by her newsroom despite criticism from government and news industry colleagues] will get her tit caught in a wringer." The *Post* didn't back off, but other news managers may have gotten the message. They let the *Post* do most of the heavy lifting before they got seriously involved in the Watergate story.

Joe McCarthy fired some flak at Ed Murrow and Fred Friendly when CBS News gave him airtime to respond to the duo's devastating assault on his Red Baiting behavior. McCarthy suggested that both journalists might well be tainted by Communist affiliations. Fortunately, for Friendly and Murrow, the tide had already turned against McCarthy. His flak missed the mark; CBS took no action against its star reporter and producer.

Flak can take a more damaging form. When TV talk show host Bill Maher took issue with Bush Administration military policy in 2002, the White House press secretary publicly questioned his patriotism and ominously suggested that Maher and others should think twice before criticizing the President. Maher's employer, ABC, got the message; they cancelled Maher's show. And there may have been more fallout than that. By equating patriotism with unquestioning support of whatever actions it took, the Bush Administration effectively silenced the news media while it lobbied Congress and the American people for war with Iraq. Who knows what truth we might have learned if journalists had been able to report objectively—to ask, for instance, if war with Iraq was an appropriate response to the attacks on the World Trade Center, the Pentagon, and a planeload of passengers over Pennsylvania in 2001—rather than being banished to the sidelines where the only acceptable (patriotic) role was as cheerleaders for an administration that built its case for war on misleading and blatantly false information. I consider the abdication of responsibility to practice professional journalism by mainstream American news media in the aftermath of September 11 to be the single most complete breakdown in truth-telling in my lifetime.

I consider the abdication of responsibility to practice professional journalism by mainstream American news media in the aftermath of September 11 to be the single most complete breakdown in truth-telling in my lifetime.

## They're Just People

Fear of flak from the powerful may not be the only reason American journalists served the public poorly after the September 11, 2001 attacks on New York City and Washington. Sometimes reporters are ordered to pull their punches by the people they work for. If their company establishes policies that restrict the truth they're allowed to tell, journalists are left with two basic choices: censor their own story or quit, as Laurie Barrett did at *Newsday*. On her way out the door, Barrett accused bottom-line focused news companies of no longer having the courage to take on business or political powers.

In practice, reporters are far more likely to acquiesce to the demands of editors than protest the shortcomings of their news organization by marching loudly and angrily out the door. It's not hard to understand why. Like most of us, they need the job, they have bills to pay, families to support. Plus, a journalist who gains a reputation for squaring off with her employers may find herself less attractive to other news companies. And it's a buyer's market out there in the twenty-first century. Mass communication and journalism schools pump out thousands of young reporters every year, many of which are eager to do serious reporting. The reality they find—low pay and a decreasing interest in pursuing potentially controversial stories—can be discouraging. And if they continue to resist meaningless assignment and attempt to pursue hard-nosed journalism, they may quickly learn another fact of life: Any news worker who veers too far from the "go along-get along" mantra can easily be replaced.

No journalist (read: employee) is big enough to withstand the forces of the firm. In 1995, even the much-vaunted Mike Wallace and *60 Minutes* backed off of the planned CBS expose of the tobacco industry when corporate lawyers decided that telling the whole truth could result in crippling lawsuits. I suspect virtually every reporter, if they're willing to be completely honest, could tell at least one story of yielding to in-house heat to modify a story or delete some of the truth contained in it rather than risk getting fired or punished. In newsrooms where I worked, we dealt with the discomfort of knowing we had sold our listeners or readers short by acknowledging that, despite our public protestations to the contrary, we all had our price and, when there seemed to be no alternative, we were willing to do whatever the company wanted as long as they paid us for it. In the end, we told ourselves, you have to make a living somehow and you can't imperil a steady income and the chances of advancement in the organization by defying your boss on a regular basis. Managers don't like employees with bad attitudes. In fact, at my last TV station, my contract forbade me to say anything negative about the firm, in house or in public. Violating that clause was grounds for dismissal.

But journalists censor themselves for another reason. They are, at the end of the day, people just like the rest of us who, perhaps with some exceptions, seek the same acceptance, respect, and companionship as anyone else. From that perspective, human nature might influence how much of the truth reporters are willing to deliver about people, events, and issues in their community.

A communication scholar named Elisabeth Noelle-Neumann describes how this social pressure can affect news reporting in a theory she calls the spiral of silence. Her basic assumption is that we all seek social acceptance as naturally as we seek the Truth about human existence. She suggests that as we move through society each day taking in information, we are also gauging other people's reactions (their attitudes and opinions) to the issues and events around us. If we sense that the majority of people we're with hold opinions that contrast with ours, we may choose to keep our thoughts to ourselves to avoid being rejected.

Noelle-Neumann believed that the need for acceptance affects news workers (who are only human, after all) even while they're in harness delivering the news. They want to be liked and respected by society (we've already noted that some journalists cling tenaciously to the status their position brings to them). If they sense that the truth they have to impart is not welcome news to their audience, they may choose not to report it, or focus the story in a way that they believe will be more acceptable to readers or viewers.

Some scholars and news professionals dismiss the spiral of silence as a misrepresentation of human nature. But, if it holds at least a little water, it might provide a partial explanation for the performance (or lack of performance) on the part of news media after the attacks on the World Trade Center in New York in 2001. Out of the terrible fear instilled by the attacks came a tremendous sense of national unity and, with considerable urging by political leaders, an extreme sense of patriotism. As the Bill Maher incident mentioned above illustrates, the general public wasn't in the mood for criticism of the United States or expressions of sympathy and understanding toward the men who staged the attacks. Perceiving that questions about our government or the motivations of the attackers were not welcome in American society just then, journalists who wanted to avoid Maher's fate may have refrained from probing some dimensions of the situation. Or, if they did have background information that might have broadened our thinking and influenced public and political reaction, they chose not to report it to avoid social rejection. As a result, much of the truth about the situation never reached the public until after important, life-threatening decisions had been made.

Noelle-Neumann used the name *spiral of silence* to describe the shrinking scope of public reflection and conversation that results from individual reluctance to challenge the tide of public opinion. The fewer facts and opinions allowed into the social conversation, the less chance any of us has of arriving at the real truth of any matter. As citizens of a democracy, we have long embraced the concept of majority rule, but if majority opinion rules over journalists who then refrain from seeking and reporting the truth about critical issues, we all lose.

## What Are They Gonna Believe?

If we're going to be fair, we can't condemn news workers for caring what society thinks of them. We all do that. And, whether some of those news workers are willing to admit it or not, they start out in life as ordinary human beings like the rest of us. But we expect reporters to train themselves to override their natural human tendency to engage in selective perception—the almost subconscious temptation to manipulate the meaning of the information they gather—so they can tell us the truth. If journalists violate our trust in their professionalism and allow personal attitudes and beliefs to dampen their commitment to objectivity, we have a right to object, which is exactly what critics have done for many years.

It's interesting to note, however, that people consuming the same news reports often reach very different conclusions about which way journalists' attitudes have slanted their stories. For instance, former CBS correspondent Bernard Goldberg loudly condemns his former colleagues in network news as dangerously biased toward liberal ideology, while noted linguist Noam Chomsky accuses major mainstream news organizations, like CBS and the *New York Times*, of intentionally reporting news from a conservative, right-wing position. Some critics point to surveys in which journalists report that their personal values tend toward the liberal end of the spectrum. Those same critics leap from that evidence to the conclusion that reporters automatically insert their liberal attitudes in the stories they write. Yet, when scholars go looking for liberal bias in the news, they have trouble finding any. (The Project for Excellence in Journalism study showing considerable expression of personal opinion in Iraq War coverage, especially on the Fox News Channel, may indicate the situation is shifting.) Where does the truth lie?

There are past and present examples of print and broadcast professionals trying to pass off their personal values and beliefs as truth. One of the most despicable instances was Father Charles Coughlin, a Catholic priest supposedly committed to telling God's Truth, who used the radio airwaves in the 1930s to spread anti-Semitic lies. Rush Limbaugh, the king of talk radio, has grown fabulously wealthy in our day delivering a steady stream of vicious, sometimes racist, and often false information, all of it biased toward his right-wing, conservative values. But Coughlin and Limbaugh are merely the most blatant examples.

A more subtle style of biased reporting emanates from the vast Christian broadcasting industry. At first glance, the "news" here looks and sounds much like mainstream journalism. But the audience needs to be aware that the anchors and reporters filter any information they get through their conservative religious beliefs before it hits the air. These broadcasters basically ask the public to surrender their judgment and accept on "faith" that the reporters are telling them what they need to know. That ideological bias eliminates any chance that the audience will receive objectively verified facts they can use in determining the truth.

It's tempting to dismiss people like Father Coughlin, Rush Limbaugh, and conservative religious ideologues as little more than propagandists who have nothing to do with real journalism. The impediment to ignoring them is the fact that millions of well-meaning, sincere seekers of truth believe what they say. And the "truth" they deliver has a serious impact on our society. Coughlin's vitriol led to racist assaults on American Jews. Historians credit Limbaugh with leading the conservative revolution that put an end to Democratic domination of national politics.

But are these examples of journalism dangerously limited by beliefs and values at all representative of the large crowd of mainstream journalists working in America today? The evidence I gathered over two decades in radio and television newsrooms is equivocal. On one hand, most of the people I worked with prided themselves on not being influenced by any religious or political doctrine or creed in doing their job. A general sense of skepticism and cynicism pervaded the atmosphere in which we labored. Politicians, business leaders, and most public officials (like the police) were, in common newsroom parlance, "tricky bastards" who commanded no allegiance from us and who needed to be watched closely to be sure they didn't pull off some scheme for their own benefit.

On the other hand, some of my Catholic colleagues, as noted earlier, expected me to report the abortion issue from the anti-abortion side. Some of our photojournalists groaned out loud when we were assigned to cover the latest anti-war demonstration at the federal courthouse. They condemned the protesters as "peaceniks" and resented having to commit airtime to people whose values so clearly conflicted with their own. And, in private conversation, virtually every person I worked with confessed to some sort of childhood religious training and at least vestiges of residual religious beliefs.

Critics, especially those who paint journalists as self-indulgent, left-leaning liberals, often accuse reporters of being godless, amoral individuals who do not share the traditional values of our society. But recent studies discredit such accusations. A 2001 study by Doug Underwood and Keith Stamm, published in *Journalism and Mass Communication Quarterly*, found that the vast majority of reporters surveyed expressed a strong, general, religious orientation; not the irreligious nature pinned on them by critics. A full seventy-two percent of those who participated in the study said religion or spirituality is important to them. More than half of those who responded claimed membership in a church or religious organization.

A 2001 study found that the vast majority of reporters surveyed expressed a strong, general, religious orientation; not the irreligious nature pinned on them by critics.

Did those religious values and experiences influence the way reporters did their job? The researchers concluded that they did, but not in the way critics predict. Journalists expressed a deep attachment to independent thinking, an essential quality if they are to engage in professional, objective truth-telling. Their bias, if it's appropriate to call it that, was in the role they saw themselves playing. Their religious values connected to a reformist impulse, a desire to help improve our society. All of the reporters in the study, those who were religious and those who weren't, strongly endorsed compassionate values; they cared about the people and the places they reported on.

The values identified by Underwood and Stamm have been circulating in the journalistic world for a very long time. New York book publisher Jesse Haney struck the first blow for integrity in reporting in 1867 in a volume entitled *Haney's Guide to Authorship.* He advises young journalists to be impartial, objective, nonpartisan, fair, and honest. In his 1890 textbook, *Steps Into Journalism,* Edwin Shuman informed young writers that modern journalism was objective. Indulging in bias and opinion, Shuman said, marked a reporter as an unsophisticated country bumpkin. When the American Society of Newspaper Editors adopted its first code of ethics in 1924, it devoted an entire section to the importance of truth and accuracy in reporting. In 1926, the Society of Professional Journalists endorsed essentially the same standards, beginning with a section encouraging professional journalists to seek truth and report it.

In 1997, with self-appointed bias police like talk radio hosts and Bernard Goldberg trashing mainstream news media from the right and left, a Committee of Concerned Journalists formed to enlist the public and reporters in reexamining what journalism was supposed to be. The committee concluded that the basic purpose of journalism is to provide information people need to be free and self-governing. And the committee offered nine principles of good journalism. Number One: Journalism's first obligation is to the truth. The committee conceded, as we've already discussed here, that the truth can be "sticky" and what qualifies as truth is often misunderstood. They observed that the focus on the bottom line had undermined journalism's credibility and warned that news workers had better address the problem or risk losing their profession.

News professionals continue calling their colleagues back to the basic task of telling people the truth. In 2003, *Columbia Journalism Review* Managing Editor Brent Cunningham told readers objectivity is increasingly important in an age of partisanship and polarization. The public needs, he wrote, "reliable reporting that tells them what is true when that is knowable, and pushes as close to the truth as possible when it is not." Television journalist Bill Moyers made the point even more forcefully in a 2005 address to the National Conference for Media Reform. He charged journalists with responsibility to act as "filters for readers and viewers, sifting the truth from the propaganda." As Ed Murrow did long ago, Moyers urged news workers not to be satisfied with simple-minded objectivity that leaves the public with little more than he said-she said. Useful objective journalism, he said, "means describing the object being reported on, including the little fibs and fantasies as well as the Big Lie of the people in power . . . to get as close as possible to the verifiable truth." Moyers went beyond the Committee of Concerned Journalists' caution that not delivering objective journalism could mean the demise of the journalistic profession. He warned that failure to tell the public the truth threatens the future of our society: "An unconscious people, an in-doctrinated people, a people fed only on partisan information and opinions that confirm their own bias, a people made morbidly obese in mind and spirit by the junk food of propaganda, is less inclined to put up a fight, to ask questions and be skeptical. That kind of orthodoxy can kill a democracy—or worse."

Moyers warned that failure to tell the public the truth threatens the future of our society.

Have these encouraging words and dire predictions produced a revolution in American journalistic practice equivalent to the introduction of objective reporting standards at the
turn of the twentieth century? Our review of the state of the
news industry in the early twenty-first century didn't turn up
much evidence of it. The public remains highly critical of news
media, print and broadcast, national and local, commercial and
public. And the industry keeps giving people more reasons to
view journalists with disdain.

The list of indiscretions and untruths is growing steadily.
Janet Cooke made up a story about a child caught in the hell
of inner-city drug activity and lost a Pulitzer Prize and her job.
The *Boston Globe* fired veteran columnist Mike Barnicle for
repeatedly fabricating stories. The *New York Times* caught and
fired Jayson Blair for the same sins. *USA Today* dumped Tom
Squitieri for plagiarism. Television host Armstrong Williams
landed in hot water when the public discovered that he failed to
disclose the fact that he took tens of thousands of dollars from
the George W. Bush Administration to plug their education ini-
tiatives on his program. Columnist Maggie Gallagher forgot to
tell her readers that she was paid more than twenty thousand
dollars to promote the same Administration's attitudes on marriage. Those are the ethical violations we know about. Who can
say how many others there are at the local or national level that
we don't know about. Ethical failures haven't managed to kill
the practice of journalism, but they have dealt a serious blow
to the public's ability to trust news media to tell them the truth.
And they raise serious questions about the values that guide
and motivate professional journalists as they do their work.

## Informed by Faith

Over the years, some people who knew I was a Christian assumed my religious values would directly affect my work as a
journalist. They seemed to think that a person of faith would
somehow do a better job with the news than a non-believer.

They often looked a bit disappointed when I told them I was confident my atheist colleague covered the news every bit as well as I did. I believed then as I do now that what makes someone a good reporter is good reporting skills and a deep commitment to providing readers, listeners, and viewers with verifiable facts about issues and events that touch their lives, information they need to know, the truth. And non-religious journalists can be just as committed to that process as people of faith.

But after years of reflection on the matter, I have come to believe that religious faith can have an important effect on the way a journalist does the job. It doesn't make you any smarter or quicker or more imposing, but it does focus your energy. Like the reporters in Underwood and Stamm's study, my encounter with religion connects me to compassionate values and generates reformist impulses. Reporting becomes more than just a job; for a person of faith, good, objective reporting is an obligation and a service. I honestly wanted to be useful to the public, to tell them the truth about their community to the best of my ability. Sloughing off and entertaining people with lighthearted or even heartwarming feature stories was not a serious option (OK, I did one now and then and I enjoyed it.) My religious faith compelled me to seek justice, to tell the truth wherever I worked. I lay no claim to having made a huge difference in my work, but I do believe I made a contribution to the cause of truth and justice.

Unfortunately, as we've now seen, the same cannot be said for much of what passes for journalism today. Commercial and political forces bearing down on news organizations and polarization of the American public by self-serving propagandists of all stripes have made it increasingly difficult for mainstream journalists to tell the hard truth and expose the official lies. As a result, it's nearly impossible for an objective, open-minded person to satisfy her need to know and

> For a person of faith, good, objective reporting is an obligation and a service.

understand what's happening in the world through commercial news media alone. We can hope, along with Bill Moyers and Brent Cunningham, that mainstream media and the people who own them will undergo a conversion experience and realize how important telling the truth is to the health of our society.

Some observers would say it's already too late; objective, truthful journalism has been sold for a higher stock dividend or profit margin. I think it will be hard to reverse the modern trend, but I'm still willing to believe it's possible. In the meantime, however, we need to know the truth and there are some alternative sources we can look to. The challenge is knowing where to look and finding the time and energy to do it. This book can't rearrange your daily schedule, but I can offer some suggestions for those willing and able to seek the truth mainstream news media are not currently willing (or able) to provide. Let's move on to chapter six.

*Chapter Six*

# How We Can Be Responsible News Consumers

> I think there ought to be a club in which preach-
> ers and journalists could come together and have
> the sentimentalism of the one matched with the
> cynicism of the other. That ought to bring them
> pretty close to the truth.
>
> • Reinhold Niebuhr

For many years, when I thought about the human beings who walked the earth in the millennia before us, I imagined them living in a simpler, less stressful world. I felt almost nostalgic for the good old days and the peaceful, pastoral existence our ancestors enjoyed before the industrial revolution upended the social structure and chained most ordinary people to the treadmill of commerce. I now know, from reading the work of archeologists and historians, that life was never that blissful for common folks. The time of their lives wasn't spent in recreational pursuits; it was dedicated to the daily struggle to survive in an often-dangerous environment, to put food on the table and a roof over their heads.

But our early relatives did have one advantage over us, it seems to me. They didn't have to work as hard as we do to find the truth about the world and its inhabitants. For thousands of years, religious leaders, the guardians of society's myths and stories and explanations, provided the answers to people's questions and guided their thoughts and actions. It was one-stop shopping and, while it may have lacked the scientific insights of modern times, it was the best Truth human beings had come up with so far and our ancestors believed it and lived by it. We have no such luxury today. The accident of birth has dropped us into a far more complex era where widespread literacy, scientific theory, technological innovation, and mass communication combine to present us with a dizzying array of information, much of it claiming to be the Truth.

> Our early relatives did have one advantage over us, it seems to me. They didn't have to work as hard as we do to find the truth about the world and its inhabitants.

Many of us still base our lives on the beliefs instilled in us by religious leaders. But we have come to depend on mass media—news media—for truth about the everyday world that we can factor into our faith in forming our sense of reality and deciding how to act. When the news arrives in so many different shapes and shades, discovering its true color is a challenging task. This book is intended as a guide for those who believe we are obligated to seek Truth, in news media and elsewhere, for ourselves and those with whom we share the planet. In this section, we offer some suggestions for working at it.

## Attitude Check

In chapters two and three, we examined the influence our beliefs and attitudes (including our religious faith) can have on our ability to accurately hear the information delivered to us in the news. Thanks to the pioneering work of Hadley Cantril and the many social and cognitive psychologists that have helped us understand how our minds work, we know we are inclined to be selective in processing information. We may avoid news that clashes with our attitudes and ideologies or seek only information that confirms what we already think. Even if we choose to expose ourselves to a news report, we may alter the journalist's intended meaning, and choose to understand the information in a way that is more compatible with our existing attitudes and beliefs. And, if we store the information in our memory, our attitudes may cause our minds to alter the information when we try to recall it later.

The hazard of selectivity in exposure, perception, and memory is that it can close our minds and prevent us from learning the real truth about important issues and events. It also reduces our potential for understanding those who do not share our attitudes and opinions. A helpful antidote is to closely examine our attitudes and understand the beliefs they're based on. We can also school ourselves in objectivity, a quality we demand from news workers, and emulate Atticus Finch by forcing ourselves to see the world through someone else's eyes and think their thoughts. If we come to the news sincerely committed to understanding information as professional journalists intend to communicate it, we move a giant step closer to finding the truth.

## Wading in the Mainstream

Getting in touch with our own attitudes and biases, and our natural tendency to expose ourselves to information that is compatible with them may shed light on the sources of news we rely on in our search for the truth. As we've already noted, most mainstream news organizations acquire reputations for reporting the news through ideological filters such as liberalism or conservatism. (We've used the term *mainstream journalism* frequently in this discussion. For the sake of clarity and common understanding, we can define it as reporting that reflects the prevalent attitudes, values, and practices of a society or group. Mainstream journalism tends to support the status quo, largely because most mainstream news media are owned by companies at least as committed to the bottom line as they are to telling the truth.)

If we commit ourselves to bridling our own biases and objectively evaluating the news we read, watch and listen to, it's important to know which way our favorite news source leans, if it leans. A little research into who owns "the press" may shed light on the editorial slant that shows up in the finished news product. We mentioned Rupert Murdoch's affirmative response when asked if owning the news (and he owns many news outlets) tempted him to impose his personal biases on the newsroom. All of the major American television news organizations are now in the hands of giant corporations. Conglomerates are building long chains of newspapers. A little digging into the people and ideologies living in the head office might partially explain why a given publication or broadcast delivers the news the way it does. The boxed material on pages 136–137 lists major mainstream news organizations, their owners, and the ideological slant generally attributed to the companies.

We may still choose to read the same newspaper or watch the same network news after we've connected the newsroom to the boardroom, but knowing that the reporting is biased to any degree tells us that the news organization is selective in its choice of stories and in its choice of facts to put in those stories. (The journalistic routines we examined in chapter five reduce the amount of information even further.) That means some of the truth won't be there. And that means, if we're trying to be objective and open-minded in our quest to know about the world we live in, we need to find other news sources to fill in the gaps.

If we compare major news sources against each other, we can see how their accounts of important events differ. We can learn a great deal of truth from those differences. Here's an example: One of the hottest political stories in the summer of 2005 involved allegations that someone in the White House exposed the identity of a covert CIA agent (a potentially criminal offense) to get revenge on her husband, a former ambassador who publicly refuted the administration's claim that Iraq tried to buy uranium for nuclear weapons. By July of that summer, a special investigation into the case was nearing completion. In those final hours, several New York newspapers reported that a person, identified only as someone who was "well briefed" in the case, claimed that White House aides had told investigators that reporters revealed the agent's name to them.

> If we're trying to be objective and open-minded in our quest to know about the world we live in, we need to find other news sources to fill in the gaps.

Two newspapers generally regarded as applying a conservative slant to their reporting (*Newsday* and Rupert Murdoch's *New York Post*) focused almost entirely on the new, anonymous assertion. Only at the end of its version did *Newsday* mention that at least one reporter claimed the President's aides revealed the agent's name. The *New York Post* included the reporters' contentions in the first two lines of its story. The Associated Press, which has long attempted to provide objective, balanced reporting for the 1,500 newspapers (with all sorts of political inclinations) who belong to its cooperative organization, ran two stories in the same time period, but did not mention the new assertion in either one. Instead, it reported on a Democratic call for Congress to investigate the leak. In that story, Senator Frank Lautenberg was quoted as saying that the lack of Congressional oversight of the White House "is dangerous for the country."

The *New York Times* (which we have already noted draws criticism for being slanted to the right and the left) reported the new assertion, but it comprised a very small part of a lengthy recap of the whole case. The *Times* summary stated flatly that someone in the White House exposed the agent and reminded

## Who Owns What And Which Way Do They Lean?

(This is a list of major American news organizations and their owners. A more complete list of major corporations and their holdings is available at www.cjr.org/tools/owners/. It's a good place to start in tracking down who owns the media outlets you rely on. Labeling a news organization as conservative, moderate, or liberal is a controversial exercise. Some news organizations may assume a particular ideological or political slant in their editorials or commentaries, yet produce fairly objective reporting in their straight-up news stories. Others may intentionally incorporate a particular viewpoint within their news. What follows is meant to provide some indication of how critics generally perceive the news companies. The categories used are: Conservative, Liberal, and Moderate, or somewhere in the middle.)

| MEDIA ORGANIZATION | OWNER | LEANING |
| --- | --- | --- |
| ABC News | Walt Disney Company | Moderate |
| *Boston Globe* | New York Times Company | Liberal and Conservative |
| CBS News | Viacom | Moderate |
| CNN | Time Warner | Moderate to Liberal |
| *Chicago Tribune* | Tribune Company of Chicago | Moderate now |
| *Christian Science Monitor* | Christian Science Publishing Society | Moderate |
| Fox News | News Corporation (Rupert Murdoch) | Conservative |
| *Houston Chronicle* | Hearst Communications, Inc. | Moderate |
| *Los Angeles Times* | Tribune Company of Chicago | Liberal |
| MSNBC | General Electric and Microsoft | Moderate to Conservative |
| *National Review* | Controlled by William F. Buckley's son | Conservative |

| MEDIA ORGANIZATION | OWNER | LEANING |
|---|---|---|
| NBC News | General Electric | Moderate |
| Nation | Washington Post Company | Liberal |
| Newsweek | Mortimer Zuckerman | Moderate |
| New York Daily News | News Corporation (Rupert Murdoch) | Conservative |
| New York Post | New York Times Company | Liberal and Conservative |
| New York Times | Knight Ridder Corporation | Moderate |
| Philadelphia Inquirer | Hearst Communications, Inc. | Moderate |
| San Francisco Chronicle | Nation Company, L.P. | Liberal |
| Washington Post | Washington Post Company | Moderate |
| Time Magazine | Time Warner | Moderate |
| U.S. News & World Report | Mortimer Zuckerman | Conservative |
| Village Voice | Controlled by investor group | Liberal |
| Wall Street Journal | Dow Jones & Co. | Conservative |
| Washington Times | Unification Church (Sun Myung Moon) | Conservative |

*Note:* You may have noticed that broadcast networks (ABC, CBS, and NBC) tend to fall in the Moderate category. That is likely the result of producing news that will attract the most viewers, which means avoiding biased reports that might alienate audience on both sides of the ideological aisle. Cable news networks (CNN, Fox News Channel, and MSNBC) have engaged in more ideologically oriented news to compete for the much smaller cable news audience. Fox News Channel, with a clearly evident conservative slant, had proven most popular among cable news viewers as of 2005.

readers that the Administration had actually backed away from the Iraq-uranium claims before someone decided to reveal the agent's identity.

The claim that reporters told White House aides the agent's name also appeared in the *Village Voice*, a liberally oriented weekly newspaper. The *Voice* article didn't advance our knowledge of what really happened any farther than the other publications, but the reporter did raise some larger issues for readers to think about. He pointed out that a growing number of news organizations, including several related to the leak story, were choosing to cooperate with investigators and reveal their confidential sources. (Refusal to do so in this case had already landed a *New York Times* reporter in jail for contempt of court.) The reporter expressed serious concern for the future of freedom of the press if the government were to take away a tool (protection of sources) that journalists have long relied on to find the truth about critical issues and events. The reporter concluded by admitting that the leak story, like many others, had grown murky and confusing, leaving journalists as well as the public "pretty much in the dark." Acknowledging the distrust many people have developed toward news media, the reporter urged his colleagues to consider confessing right at the top of hard-to-pin-down stories how much they don't know. Such candor, the reporter wrote, will breed credibility. I have to admit, whether or not I am ideologically sympathetic with this journalist and his publication, his honesty in approaching the task leaves me inclined to pay closer attention to what he has to say.

Have we nailed down the whole truth about this issue by examining multiple versions of the latest development? Obviously not, but we are now in possession of a great deal more information than we would have been if we stopped after reading only one of these newspapers. Knowing how each paper treated the story helps us assume a more objective position from which to monitor future developments. And we are newly sensitized to the pressure people in power can apply to those who gather and report the news. We might also be curious to know who suggested, well into a federal investigation of the leak, the idea that it was reporters, not the White House, that blew the agent's cover in the first place. We might also ask what motivated the anonymous source to inject a new version of events into the conversation so late in the game. And why did certain reporters feature the information prominently in their stories while others downplayed or ignored it? As ordinary people increasingly dependent on news media to know what's happening in our world, we should care if news companies are surrendering our right to a free press by allowing government or anyone else to control how they do their jobs.

## Do a Little Digging

We can also assume more responsibility for informing ourselves about what's going on and what it means. Through the Internet and traditional reference sources such as books and magazine and newspaper archives we can dig up background information, additional facts and figures, that may lead us closer to the truth. A few hours online or in the local library could provide answers to questions the news media, for whatever reasons, may not have addressed as thoroughly as they could have or not at all.

The case of the outed CIA agent provides a good example. When the story first broke, most news reports stated as fact that publicly identifying a covert agent was a criminal offense, not to mention that it put the agent and anyone she worked with in other countries in grave danger. Much later, as the special prosecutor's investigation appeared to be drawing to a close, the language changed. News accounts reported that whoever leaked this agent's name might not have broken the law. What were we supposed to believe? What's the truth?

A quick search of the Internet turned up the exact wording of the law in question, the Intelligence Identities Protection

Act (U.S. Code Title 50. Section 421) passed in 1982. The law imposes fines and prison terms up to ten years on anyone who intentionally reveals the identity of a covert agent. But legal experts have very different opinions of what it really means.

Two lawyers who helped write the law said it wasn't intended to nail a government employee who carelessly revealed the identity of a covert agent. One of the authors (a deputy assistant attorney general under the Republican Reagan Administration) believed the 2003 leak wasn't a crime, according to a July, 2005 report in the *Los Angeles Times*. But a former CIA general counsel asked why the Justice Depart would bother to investigate the leak if there wasn't evidence of wrongdoing.

News accounts in the summer of 2005 emphasized the skepticism expressed by one of the lawyers who helped write the law, often without tying that view to the person who expressed it. Digging around and finding out that she worked for an earlier Republican-run Justice Department made me question her motives in dismissing allegations of criminal activity against another Republican Administration. In this case, exploring the background helped me put the story in a clearer context. Again, we haven't managed to establish the exact truth, but we now have more knowledge to use in analyzing future developments.

## Triangulating from Alternative Sources

Mainstream media companies have managed to monopolize much of our Truth-seeking time over the years by marketing themselves as the most knowledgeable, comprehensive sources of information available. But that hasn't discouraged a host of smaller organizations, some of them religiously affiliated, and collectively known as *alternative media*, from reporting on the issues and events that shape our lives. Alternative media, often written from a point of view, can be a useful source of information that we can contrast with mainstream sources. Smaller, often noncommercial, alternative media give voice to sources that mainstream media consider beneath their notice. If we triangulate on a topic using the information provided by mainstream and alternative media, we may be able to guide ourselves closer to the truth.

> If we triangulate on a topic using the information provided by mainstream and alternative media, we may be able to guide ourselves closer to the truth.

Some of these groups set up shop to serve as watch dogs of the media themselves and publish critiques documenting major media bias, collusion with government, and failure to cover stories we need to know about. An outstanding example on the progressive or liberal side of the political line is Fairness & Accuracy in Reporting (FAIR), which publishes a bimonthly magazine entitled *Extra!* FAIR also operates a website at www. fair.org. In the March/April issue of *Extra!,* an investigative reporter confessed that most of his best stories began with a tip from frustrated editors at mainstream newspapers who can't interest their superiors in what they believe are important issues.

Another dedicated group in the liberal camp is Truthout, which publishes original reporting and reprints articles from alternative and mainstream media online at www.truthout.org. Truthout frequently features the work of journalists such as Seymour Hersh, who writes investigative, background articles for *New Yorker* magazine. While mainstream media rode the patriotic wave after the September 11, 2001 attacks, Hersh and his colleagues at the *New Yorker* were already at work digging out information to help us understand how something like 9/11 could happen.

We don't have space here to list all of the alternative voices available today (see the box on pp. 142–45), but they aren't hard

## Guide To Alternative News Sources

Media criticism does exist in America. But by and large, it is not citizen-based criticism designed to make media a better source of information in a democracy. Instead, it is a cynical manipulation of the discourse designed to silence even the mildest dissent.                        • Robert McChesney and John Nichols

*(The organizations listed below have all made a public commitment to "police" mainstream news media and their coverage of important issues and events. They can be very helpful in the search for truth. Be advised that some of these groups are ideologically based and the information they provide may be influenced by those attitudes and beliefs.)*

**Fairness & Accuracy in Reporting (FAIR):** In the organization's own words: "FAIR is a media watch organization offering constructive criticism in an effort to correct media imbalance. We advocate for media access on behalf of those constituencies in our society that do not have the wealth to purchase their own TV stations or daily newspapers. We scrutinize media practices that slight public interest, peace, and minority viewpoints. All of us who founded FAIR [in 1986] have media backgrounds. Our sympathies are with the working press. We do not view reporters, editors and producers as our enemy. Nor do we hunt for conspiracies. The villain we see is not a person or group, but a historical trend: the increasing concentration of the U.S. media in fewer and fewer corporate hands." Online at www.fair.org, also publishes *Extra!* bi-monthly.

**Truthout (www.truthout.org):** Truthout (TO) is staffed by former journalists and publishes their original work along with reprints of stories published elsewhere (including mainstream media) that the editors consider on target. The editors explain its origins: "We started TO in the aftermath of the 2000 Presidential election hoping that we could . . . have some small impact on the dialog, and maybe . . . try to restore a little integrity. Today TO is visited more than 4 million times per month by readers seeking the straight story and wanting to be involved in building a better tomorrow."

**New Yorker magazine:** Publishes investigative and in-depth articles that provide important background information about the issues, events, and individuals impacting our lives.

**Mother Jones magazine:** There's no question about the motivation behind this publication, as the editors explain: "Mother Jones is an independent nonprofit whose roots lie in a commitment to social justice implemented through first rate investigative reporting. . . . Mother Jones' founders envisioned a magazine devoted to a new brand of socially conscious journalism—one that took on corporate as well as political power [through investigative reporting]." Online at www.motherjones.com and in print.

**Z Magazine:** Clearly a progressive publication as its founders explain, "Z Magazine was founded in 1987, by two of the cofounders of South End Press. The name was inspired by the movie Z, directed by Costa-Gavras, that tells the story of repression and resistance in Greece, [hence, the magazine is] dedicated to resisting injustice, defending against repression, and creating liberty. It sees the racial, gender, class, and political dimensions of personal life as fundamental to understanding and improving contemporary circumstances; and it aims to assist activist efforts for a better future."

**www.zmag.org/altmediaresources.htm:** Extensive listing of progressive or liberal print and online publications offering an alternative take on the events of the day, compiled by the staff of Z Magazine.

**IPPN www.ippn.ws/:** Another index of progressive publications. IPPN stands for International Progressive Publications Network.

Interestingly, IPPN monitors both alternative and mainstream publications. Website permits quick location of media sources in most parts of the world. Reading or seeing world events reported by journalists who live there can be an eye-opening experience.

**Jay's Leftist and "Progressive" Internet Resources Directory (www.neravt.com/left/):** Jay makes no bones about who this site is for: "A Web Portal for all Good People around Planet Earth who are anti-War, anti-Imperialist, anti-Racist, anti-Sexist, and anti-Homophobic and who want to Fight Back and build together a Better World."

**Project Censored (www.projectcensored.org/):** An ongoing media research project housed at Sonoma State University in California. As its organizers explain, "Project Censored . . . tracks the news published in independent journals and newsletters. From these, Project Censored compiles an annual list of 25 news stories of social significance that have been overlooked, under-reported or self-censored by the country's major national news media." Publishes yearly hard-copy edition of top 25 censored stories. Not afraid to point fingers at large, powerful government and corporate entities.

**Media Research Center (www.MediaResearch.org):** Calling itself America's media watchdog, MRC began in 1987 when, as organizers explain, "a group of young determined conservatives set out to not only prove—through sound scientific research—that liberal bias in the media does exist and undermines traditional American values, but also to neutralize its impact on the American political scene." Monitors all major (mainstream) print and broadcast news daily.

**Times Watch (www.TimesWatch.org):** The name of the organization tells the story. A sub-group of the Media Research Center, Times Watch is "dedicated to documenting and exposing the liberal political agenda of the *New York Times*." The group's website acknowledges the *New York Times* as the most influential newspaper in the world.

**Free Market Project (FreeMarketProject.org):** Another effort sponsored by the Media Research Center, the genesis of which organizers explain this way: "Before the Media Research Center (MRC) launched the Free Market Project (FMP) in 1992, there was no entity in America devoted solely to analyzing and exposing the anti-free enterprise culture of the media. With the FMP in operation, that void has been filled." An interesting counterweight to all of the progressive and liberal talk of social justice and the disadvantaged.

**Accuracy In Media (AIM) (www.aim.org):** A generally conservative leaning group now run by the son of the founder, Reed Irvine. AIM describes itself as "a non-profit, grassroots citizen's watchdog of the news media that critiques botched and bungled news stories and sets the record straight on important issues that have received slanted coverage." AIM has been around since 1969.

**Alternative Press Index (www.altpress.org):** This is another venerable source of alternative media. It began the same year as Accuracy In Media with the expressed goal of being "a non-profit collective dedicated to providing access to and increasing public awareness of the alternative press." The index can be accessed online or acquired in hard copy. The website also indexes more than 400 alternative voices reachable on the Internet.

to find. *Mother Jones* magazine, a progressive voice itself, also links to an extensive index of organizations at www.zmag.org/altmediaresources.htm. A very expressive voice on the conservative side of the aisle is the Media Research Center (MRC) which for seventeen years has claimed the title of America's

Media Watchdog, dedicated to "documenting, exposing and neutralizing" the left-wing press. MRC is upfront about its agenda; it runs three websites: www.MediaResearch.org, www.TimesWatch.org, and www.FreeMarketProject.org.

Most major religious denominations also address the issues of the day, and many of them operate web sites and publish magazines in which they report the news from their particular perspective, conservative or liberal, Christian, Jewish, or Muslim. We would hope that religious groups would adhere to a high ethical standard of honesty and objectivity in dealing with the news, and we may welcome a news treatment produced by someone who shares our beliefs and values, but we need to be cautious in examining their conclusions as to what constitutes the truth. To uncover any built-in bias, it's a good idea to check out the background of any alternative media just as we've suggested doing for mainstream media.

## Blog, Blog, Blog

Technologically hip readers will have noticed by now that, even in a discussion of alternative media, I neglected to mention one of the latest Internet innovations—the blog (short for Web log). Blogs began as public journals in which individuals shared their thoughts about "whatever" and invited readers to respond. Over time, some bloggers have come to see themselves as news reporters. In a couple of instances blogs have actually contributed verifiable information to the public conversation. But there's a problem here.

Bloggers do not commit themselves to the same code of ethics as professional journalists, and most of them have no training in objective reporting. As a result, bloggers and journalists have very different ideas about how we discover the truth. Rather than learning reporting skills and applying them to extract the truth from issues and events, bloggers publish unverified information (opinions, rumors, allegations) and expect reaction from multiple readers to whittle the information into truth. There is little or no regard for the damage that can be done by publishing unsubstantiated allegations.

The strange case of the Bush National Guard memos illustrates the point. In 2004, CBS News broadcast a report accusing President George W. Bush of failing to fulfill his military obligations to the Guard. The story was based, in part, on several memos, purportedly written by Bush's commander. An avowedly right-wing blog immediately claimed that the memos were forgeries, supporting its allegations with testimony from "experts." The blog's assertions triggered an independent investigation at CBS, which led to the dismissal of four veteran news professionals and Dan Rather's early departure from the anchor chair.

The uproar drowned out input from other "experts" who argued that the memos looked real to them, and it obscured later speculation that the memos may in fact be legitimate. More important, the volume of the right-wing condemnation of CBS also prevented most of the public from hearing the Guard commander's former secretary state that the information in the questionable documents was in fact correct. The *New York Times* quoted her as saying, "It looks like someone may have read the originals and put that together." Just another political tempest in a teapot, you might be thinking. I believe it's much more serious than that. Beyond the immediate damage to the careers of four well-respected news professionals, the original blogging (not the product of professional journalistic practices) distracted the nation's attention from the larger story: an alleged cover-up (possibly including shredding of official documents) to hide the truth about an incumbent President's performance in the National Guard.

Bloggers are free to say whatever they want to say, and, short of lawsuits, they can't be held accountable for any of it. Perhaps bloggers will mature into responsible journalists who can be trusted to provide the sort of factual, verifiable truth we expect

> Perhaps bloggers will mature into responsible journalists who can be trusted to provide the sort of factual, verifiable truth we expect from news media.

from news media. But for the moment, I think they pose more of a hazard than a help to truth-seekers.

We've covered a lot of territory in our discussion of news media and their uneven performance in bringing us the truth we seek in understanding our world and our place in it. I don't blame you if you're thinking you don't have the time and energy to assume so much responsibility for winnowing the daily crop of news to find the Truth. But I believe that God stands ready to support us if we are willing to make the effort. Let's move on to chapter seven for some suggestions on how we can read, hear, and view the news and respond to it through the filter of faith.

# Chapter Seven

# Let Us Think (and Pray)

> Truth is the best armor to fight evil in life. I will
> tread the path of life with the torch of truth ever
> ablaze in my hand. From dawn to dusk, I will be
> true both in words and in deeds.
>
> ▪ Zarathustra

This book is my sincere attempt to create an aid we can all use in our daily confrontation with a tidal wave of mass mediated news and information in our quest for Truth. Like our prehistoric ancestors or the twentieth-century Americans who endured two world wars and a devastating economic depression we have an urgent need to know about the world. And it is my belief that being in touch with how our minds and news media work will improve our chances of separating the truthful wheat from the often biased and incomplete media chaff. But a book can't digest the news for us. We still have to do the heavy lifting ourselves; we have to think critically and objectively about the information we take in.

That theme—thinking for ourselves—has flowed just beneath the surface of this entire discussion. It emboldened me to tackle, in my own limited fashion, the formidable, age-old question: What is Truth? It's the characteristic that Hadley Cantril found in listeners who did not panic when Martians invaded the earth (Cantril called it critical ability). It's the skill needed to analyze our attitudes and beliefs and understand how they impact our perception of whatever information we take in through our senses. It's an essential weapon in our Truth-seeking arsenal. The pace of modern life may leave us feeling too tired to commit the time and energy required for thoughtful, reflective consumption of the news. But the results may be enlightening and inspiring. And those of us who are in touch with a higher power can draw on that to help us.

> The pace of modern life may leave us feeling too tired to commit the time and energy required for thoughtful, reflective consumption of the news. But the results may be enlightening and inspiring.

## Living the Truth

I believe Christ expects us to make an effort to know the truth about our world. In John 8:31–38, Jesus is in conversation with people identified as "Jews who *had* believed in him." Directly addressing their present doubts, he tells them that if they continue to heed his message (the *Logos* or Word of God, his revelation of the nature of God), they will be true, genuine disciples. That commitment, Jesus tells them, will allow them to know the Truth, and that Truth will make them free. The Truth in this case, according to biblical scholars, is not simply general knowledge, as we might expect to receive from modern news media, but the revelation of God through Christ. And the freedom to be won is freedom from sin. The word "sin" may strike us as a bit old fashioned in our post-Freudian world. But if we understand it to mean living our lives in disregard of the relationship God seeks with us and the relationship that God through Christ urges us to seek with the totality of God's created world, the need to monitor our society and the world through news media pops back into the picture.

The same biblical scholars who define the word "truth" in

John 8:32 as divine revelation go on to suggest that the evidence that we "know" this Truth is not simply mouthing the words or quoting Bible verses. What Jesus was encouraging the doubters of his time and those of us who follow them in history to do is to let God's Truth direct the way we live our lives. We are evading the issue if we ask: What does a life lived in God's Truth look like? From the Old Testament through the New Testament, the message is constant: Love God and love your neighbor as yourself. Care for the disadvantaged and seek justice for all. How do we know about our neighbors and how do we know who's disadvantaged and how do we know where oppression and injustice are raging in our global community? In the twenty-first century, the major source of information is the news media.

> How do we know where oppression and injustice are raging in our global community? In the twenty-first century, the major source of information is the news media.

But after examining the way the news comes together, we may be a bit reluctant to accept what's proffered to us each day as the Truth. What are we to do? One suggestion is to approach the news with the same prayerful attitude biblical scholars bring to the study of sacred texts (this is essentially a very specific application of critical thinking). We may find ourselves better able to sift out the junk, the bias, the outright falsehoods, and find meaning we would miss with too brief an exposure to the information.

This isn't some sort of mysticism. When it happens in the study of sacred writing, scholars call it illumination. It occurs when scholars approach the text both critically and prayerfully, seeking divine guidance in their quest to extract truth from the text. The potential for it to happen is part of the reason rabbis encourage faithful Jews to study the Torah or Christian leaders encourage believers to read and reread the Bible. It seems appropriate to consider today's dominant source of information (truth)—news media—in the same thoughtful way, asking God to help us see what's actually there and to help us hold at bay any preexisting biases that are part of our daily consciousness. The truth we find through this process can translate directly into a clearer understanding of how we should live our lives. Here are some suggestions that might enhance your truth-seeking.

## Media Use Survey

Before we launch into an analysis of the latest news, it might be useful to take stock of both our attitudes toward the news and our consumption habits. Try answering these questions:

1. What news media do you have contact with on a regular basis?
2. How much time do you spend with newspapers, magazines, radio, television, the Internet? (Logging your news media use for a week might be helpful in answering this question.)
3. Which specific news media do you favor? Identify them by name (for example, the *New York Times*, WGN Radio, *CBS Evening News*, CNN On-Line, *New Yorker* magazine, the *Nation*, *National Review*, a local newspaper, TV station, radio station, website).
4. Which level of reporting interests you most: local, national, international?
5. Why do you bother to read/listen to/watch the news?
6. How much do you trust the news media, in general? How much do you trust the particular news media you consume on a regular basis?
7. Does the information you receive from news media inform and serve your goals as a Christian? As a human being?

## The Bias Test

Select a current national or international story (preferably one with a controversial moral or political nature) and compare the treatment of that story by a variety of news organizations. You can access most national newspapers online, and TV networks often post the script of their stories on line, too. First of all, ask yourself how important this story is based on your personal values and priorities. Then notice what aspect of the story the reporter mentions first. Compare the facts presented in the entire story. Does information left out by some of the news organizations or put in by only some of the organizations suggest anything about the views held by the reporter or the company she works for? Read each sentence closely. Does the journalist identify the source of each bit of information? Are there any statements that are obviously opinion that are not attributed to someone other than the reporter? How much do the various accounts differ? How much is the same? Do you have questions about the story that the reporter hasn't answered? Does putting all of the accounts together provide a clearer picture of the issue? Would you be concerned about people of faith accepting any of the versions you've looked at as the truth? Could any of the reports mislead people and influence their attitudes or actions in a harmful way?

## Testing Local Options

Pick what you believe to be an important issue or controversy in your local community or your state. How many newspaper versions of the story can you find? Is the story running on the radio? How many of your local television stations are paying attention to the story? Compare the accounts from as many news organizations as you can find. Any signs of bias? Unattributed assertions? What do you know about the sources who are identified? Does it appear the reporter has made a serious effort to be objective, fair, and balanced? If you have only one newspaper account to examine, does that raise any concerns for you?

## News About Government, Social Issues, Injustice and the Disadvantaged

If we are to be true disciples of Christ, we must inform ourselves about the needs of our brothers and sisters at home and abroad. Your church or religious group may be involved in responding to human suffering in a number of places around the world. How did you become aware of the problems—through news media? How much time and attention do the news media you consume devote to such things? Count the number of stories in one edition of the newspaper you read or the TV news you watch that report on the conduct of government, or social and justice issues, domestic or foreign. By contrast, how many stories are there about violent or bizarre crimes, feature stories, new business openings, executive promotions, professional or collegiate sports, or syndicated material like TV listings or film reviews? News companies are increasingly fearful that we are not interested in the plight of the suffering or the humdrum turning of the wheels of government. But, as disciples of Christ, as part of twenty-first-century society, we need to know. Some journalists understand this. In the 2005 Red Smith Lecture in Journalism at the University of Notre Dame, *New Yorker* magazine's outstanding communication correspondent Ken Auletta told the audience "journalists and their editors and the people who sign our checks have to be willing to risk boring our audience to report on dry but vital subjects like budget deficits or underfunded

> News companies are increasingly fearful that we are not interested in the plight of the suffering or the humdrum turning of the wheels of government. But, as disciples of Christ we need to know.

Social Security." If our news sources are not providing this critical service, we should demand that they start. Or, as I suggest
in chapter five, we need to find alternative news sources to fill
in the widening gaps in mainstream coverage.

## Illumination and Inspiration

Let me give a personal example of what prayerful attention to
the news can do. For many years, I have turned to the Sunday
*New York Times* for a comprehensive report on what's happening around the world. On one particular Sunday, I was struck
by how many stories I was reading that detailed political or
ethnic violence in parts of the world I knew little about. In the
weeks that followed, I started counting the number of conflicts
reported by the *Times*. Often the number was well into double
digits. The stories, written in standard journalistic form and
often only a couple of paragraphs long, usually included some
explanation for the violence and an estimate of the number of
victims. The brief accounts weren't enough to give me a clear
understanding of what was going on, but they were more than
enough to raise in my mind images of ordinary people, struggling to understand the world and survive just like the rest of
us, maimed or snuffed out by those with evil intentions. The
injustice of such violence clashed with the values instilled in
me by my faith and my nation, and spurred me to keep those
people, my brothers and sisters in humanity, in my thoughts
and prayers and to lend my support to organizations, religious
or secular, committed to the cause of peace in our world. I am
under no illusion that my increased sensitivity to the world
community will put an end to injustice, but I feel more human
and more humane joining hands with others who are simi-
larly enlightened. I feel empowered and obligated to speak out
against such injustice wherever it takes place, no matter who
is responsible for it, including my own country. And I believe
it would not have struck home as forcefully for me if I had not

taken the time to engage in thoughtful, reflective reading of the basic information in the paper.

## Sin Boldly: Be Aggressive

The more time we spend thinking critically about the information we receive from mainstream news media, the more incomplete and confusing their coverage of important issues and events may seem to be. We may find ourselves wishing we had more to work with in assessing the truth of a situation. One option for meeting that need to know, as suggested earlier, is to seek alternative media sources committed to getting the full truth out about issues that effect our lives and our planet. But that avenue still leaves us dependent on someone else, albeit someone committed to professional journalistic standards, to process the available information and decide which part to share with us. My advice to those willing to take the risk is to engage in a little direct truth-seeking.

> My advice to those willing to take the risk is to engage in a little direct truth-seeking.

In one of his oft-quoted comments, the Christian reformer Martin Luther advised a friend, "Sin boldly." Luther went on to express his devout belief that no matter how brazenly we indulge our temptation to sin, the grace of God is powerful enough to defeat it. With apologies to Luther for adapting his sentiments, I believe we should "sin boldly" in our efforts to learn the truth; we can be aggressive in pursuing the information we need to know, demanding to see important records and documents, having the audacity to call individuals connected to an important issue or event and ask the questions we need answers to. Any offense those sources take over an ordinary person engaging in practices generally monopolized by professional journalists is more than outweighed by the information—hopefully truth—we gain in the process. If the people involved are on the public payroll, they have an obligation to answer our questions. They don't have the right to be offended or push us away.

I know from experience with my friends that many people shy away from the type of up-close-and-personal encounters required by the newsgathering process. But I also know how many times during my reporting career I was amazed to discover how much I could find out simply by picking up the phone or walking into an office and asking my questions. I also learned a lot by calling or visiting the reference desk at the library and admitting I was clueless about a situation or an issue. Wonderful reference librarians practically stood on their heads to help me find what I needed to know. All I had to do was pluck up my courage and swallow my pride and ask.

## Challenge the News

We can also question the news media. If we suspect them of slanting their stories we should call them on it. They probably won't like it if we do; as we noted earlier, they have their pride and their feelings, too. They may attempt to wrap themselves in the First Amendment and say freedom of the press means they report the news as they see it. We shouldn't let them get away with that. The First Amendment was written for us, too. It's supposed to guarantee that those who know the truth can share it with the rest of us without fear of reprisals from the King.

Many times, during my years in the newsroom, viewers came to me with complaints about the way a story had been handled *or* ignored. I always urged them to contact my company and let our managers know how they felt. News media, especially of the commercial variety, can't survive if people don't buy the paper or turn on the radio. That gives us some influence over them. Professional journalists, committed to the industry's code of ethics, should want to do the job right in the first place. (And I believe many of them do.) If they fall short, we should demand that they do it right, hold them accountable. And if they refuse or management restricts them, we should apply leverage by boycotting their products. Or abandon them entirely and seek other sources of truth.

## Truth, Freedom, and Love

This book began as an effort to provide people with some practical advice in ferreting out truth in the news product delivered by mass media. I hope it has done that. But, along the way, it occurred to me that it might make another contribution to society. We live in abrasive times, times of severe polarization. Nations threaten nations, people condemn each other's ideologies, talking heads on shout TV scream at each other from opposite ends of the political or values spectrum. In chapter three, I urged readers to get in touch with their own biases and to work toward an open, objective mindset before we tried to evaluate the performance of the news media. What struck me as I wrote that section was that striving toward openness and understanding might not only improve our ability to determine what ails the news business, but also move us away from our ideological polarization and closer to each other. I imagined that the shrillness of the conversation might be tempered by the reminder that we are, in the end, all in this world together, no matter how many ways we find to separate ourselves. I believe the Atticus Finch approach could work for all of us, and should work for those who profess allegiance to a God whose principle instruction to humankind is to love one another and seek justice. It seems to me we can get a "two-fer" out of this process. If we take control of and responsibility for our own minds and our communication environment, we will know more of the Truth and that Truth will help free us to live a life of true discipleship in Christ.

# Study Guide

## Questions for Reflection and Discussion:

*Chapter One*

1. Does this discussion of truth cover all the bases? Can you think of other sources of truth? How does the Truth you know through faith connect to the truth you learn from the secular, scientific world?

2. Do you accept news media as a valid source of the truth you need to know?

*Chapter Two*

1. To what extent does the Magic Bullet Theory ring true to you today? What sort of effect do you think mass media can have on us as children or adults?

2. Bring to mind an experience you've had in which your prior knowledge and religious beliefs influenced your ability to accurately perceive the world around you.

*Chapter Three*

1. Try the Atticus Finch method. Think of a person whose words and actions you can't understand or even find offensive. How do you feel when you try to "walk around in his (or her) skin" and see the world through their eyes? How does that help you get in touch with your own attitudes and beliefs?

2. Recall particular instances when you allowed your most cherished beliefs to be confronted by thoughts and attitudes

that challenge them. Give Milton's approach a try. List your
most basic religious and social beliefs. Then try to think of arguments someone who doesn't share your beliefs might make
against them. How would you defend these bedrock elements
of your faith and sense of reality?

3. Consider how objective you are when you read the news
or watch it on TV. Be honest with yourself: Can you detect any
tendency on your part to be selective in terms of exposure to,
perception of, or memory of the news you consume?

*Chapter Four*

1. How does this brief history square with your perceptions
of American journalism?

2. In what ways and to what extent do you trust today's news
media to report the truth?

*Chapter Five*

1. A survey in 2005 found that public broadcasting, radio
and television, was the most trusted news source in the United
States, ahead of newspapers and commercial television news.
Do you agree with that assessment? Why or why not?

2. Does this chapter's discussion of the pressures and constraints under which professional journalists labor make you
more or less sympathetic to them?

3. Given the routines and stresses (including increasing
commercial pressure) under which journalists work today, how
well do you think they're doing at telling us the truth about our
world?

*Chapter Six*

1. How often do you read alternative news media? How much
do you trust their version of things that happen, say, compared
with the mainstream media?

2. To test whether or not alternative media can help us in our search for the truth, pick a controversial issue attracting lots of media attention (a Supreme Court nomination or gay marriage legislation would be examples). Collect stories on this issue from several mainstream media (print, broadcast, or Internet) and from several alternative media (choose a couple from the list on pages 142–45). Compare the facts and opinions expressed in the different versions of the story. Can you discard any of the information as clearly biased? Do the alternative media provide any perspectives you find useful, from a faith and values perspective?

*Chapter Seven*

Questions for Reflection and Discussion are built into the text to encourage readers to synthesize what they've been reading and thinking about and move toward implementing a deeper, more reflective and critical approach to finding truth in news media. See pages 152 and 159–60.

# For Further Reading:

## History of News Media

*Beyond Belief: The American Press And The Coming Of The Holocaust, 1933-1945* by Deborah E. Lipstadt (Simon & Schuster Adult Publishing Group, 1993).

The author seeks to understand how a disaster of such magnitude as The Holocaust failed to find its way onto the front page of American newspapers and into the public discourse before the Nazis had carried out their genocide against the Jews of Europe. She identifies three major factors that influenced journalistic treatment of reports coming out of Germany and elsewhere: skepticism triggered by the memory of false reports surrounding World War One, a smokescreen of denials issued by both American and German business and political leaders, and the overshadowing effect of American military involvement in World War Two.

*God Willing? Political Fundamentalism in the White House, the "War on Terror" and the Echoing Press* by David Domke (Pluto, 2004).

This book examines how the Bush Administration capitalized on the fear engendered by the September 11, 2001 terrorist attacks to impose a "political fundamentalism" on America. Domke documents how media (by unquestioning repetition of the government line) helped the executive branch shut down serious conversation about the meaning of the attacks and the direction of the nation's response to them.

*Mightier Than the Sword: How the News Media Have Shaped American History* by Roger Streitmatter (Westview Press, 1998).

Streitmatter uses fourteen snapshots of American history to illustrate how the performance of news media influenced American values, politics, and the functioning of our society. He applauds the positive contributions of journalists and provides evenhanded criticism of their shortcomings. Readers come away from this book with a clearer understanding of the ebb and flow of journalistic standards of truth telling as the American experiment in democracy unfolded.

## News Professionals on News Media

*Bad News: The Decline of Reporting, the Business of News, and the Danger to Us All* by Tom Fenton (Regan, 2005).

Longtime CBS staffer Fenton stands up to loudly protest the breaching of the wall between the news department and the sales department by commercial and corporate influences. He issues an urgent call for a major reform of broadcast journalism: "We need more and better news. Our lives depend on it."

*Feet to the Fire: The Media After 9/11* edited by Kristin Borjesson (Prometheus, 2005).

Borjesson presents the challenge faced by American broadcast and print reporters in the aftermath of the September 11, 2001 terrorist attacks on the United States through extensive interviews with journalists themselves. Their responses help us understand how the government used the disaster and the fear it engendered to restrict journalists in their watchdog role and manipulate them into propagating pro-administration views.

*Into the Buzzsaw: Leading Journalists Expose the Myth of a Free Press* edited by Kristina Borjesson (Prometheus, 2004).

This is Borjesson's attempt to expose the shortcomings of mainstream journalism through the words of the practitioners themselves. The book includes accounts of important stories rejected, gutted through censorship, or drastically downplayed, written by contributors including CBS anchor Dan Rather and MSNBC reporter Ashleigh Banfield. Readers get an inside look at how decisions are made in the major news organizations claiming to serve the public interest today.

*Media Circus: The Trouble with America's Newspapers* by Howard Kurtz (Crown Publishing Group, 1994).

Kurtz, a longtime staffer at *The Washington Post*, presents a straightforward expose of the diminishing power of the press since the Watergate scandal. He documents the slide into tabloid style reporting and infotainment, and chides his colleagues across the board for focusing too much on the personal lives of celebrities and too little on issues and events that deeply affect the American people. Kurtz also offers suggestions for rescuing newspapers from their current sorry state.

## The Economics and Politics of News Media

*Breaking the News: How the Media Undermine American Democracy* by James M. Fallows (Knopf Publishing Group, 1996).

*Library Journal* observed that Fallows's book tells us how the media give us the truth, the whole truth, and nothing but the truth as they want us to see it. He addresses two questions: What's wrong with American news media and what can be done about it? To the first question, Fallows responds that the way media report the news today encourages us to believe we can do nothing to influence the course of events in our society. He addresses the second question by offering concrete proposals for improving the situation.

*Manufacturing Consent: The Political Economy of the Mass Media* by Edward S. Herman and Noam Chomsky (Pantheon Books, 2002).

Through a number of case studies and in fairly academic language, the authors support their contention that American government and big business have long since joined forces to control what we read, see, and hear. Working from an essentially Marxist point of view, they argue that the news media are complicit in maintaining power and control in the hands of the financial and political elite. And no media cow is considered sacred. Chomsky and Herman include the venerable *New York Times* in their list of culprits.

*The New Media Monopoly* by Ben Bagdikian (Beacon Press, 2004).

Back in 1983, Ben Bagdikian wrote this book to warn Americans that the consolidation of news media ownership in a dwindling number of corporate hands threatened to narrow the scope of public discussion of important issues. At the time, critics labeled him an alarmist. This revised edition confirms that the number of corporations controlling most of our news media has dropped from fifty to five and Bagdikian still argues that has had a drastic effect on the marketplace of ideas.

## Attitudes and Beliefs

*The Psychology of Attitude and Attitude Change* by Alice Eagly, Shelly Chaiken, and Dawn Youngblood (Wadsworth, 1993).

This is a fairly scholarly treatment of the issues and research related to how we form and change our attitudes and beliefs. But it touches on issues important to people of faith, such as the roots of racism and how we can address it through attitude change. It also examines the selectivity we are inclined to practice as a result of the attitudes and beliefs we hold, and the impact of attitudes on our behavior.

## Bias and News Media

*Bias: A CBS Insider Exposes How the Media Distort the News* by Bernard Goldberg (HarperCollins Publishers, 2003).
Goldberg is so convinced that conservative accusations of liberal media bias are true that he claims he had no choice but to write this book and expose it. He argues that the left-wing slant is so pervasive that it affects every decision made by professional journalists at CBS News. Goldberg names names and cites specific instances along the road as liberal bias rubbed out fairness, balance, and integrity in network television news.

*The Language of Empire: Abu Ghraib and the American Media* by Lila Rajiva (Monthly Review Press, 2005).
In her first book, independent journalist Lila Rajiva documents how, in her estimation, mainstream American news media coverage of the Iraq war has dulled, rather than sharpened, the American public conscience. She hammers on propagandist radio and TV talkers Sean Hannity and Rush Limbaugh, and argues that mainstream media coverage of the war has been shamefully racist. In the larger view, she suggests that the frames used by American media to report on the war better serve corporate than democratic interests.

*Slick Spins and Fractured Facts: How Cultural Myths Distort the News* by Caryl Rivers (Columbia University Press, 1996).
Who says you can't address serious problems in a humorous way. With a combination of wit and persuasive argument, Rivers indicts the major players in news media—upper-middle class whites—for indulging their self interests and ideologies to produce a news product that perpetuates gender, race, and class stereotypes from one generation to the next. In the process, Rivers encourages us to question our own assumptions and offers the hopeful prediction that future journalists can be more inclusive in their understanding of the news.

*Unreliable Sources: A Guide to Detecting Bias in News Media* by Martin Lee and Norman Solomon (Kensington Publishing Corporation, 1991).

Lee and Solomon both have connections to the progressive media watchdog group, Fairness and Accuracy in Reporting (FAIR). More than a decade after its original publication, it's still a helpful handbook for dissecting mainstream news media treatment of important public issues from taxes to war to social security. The authors argue that mainstream media are reluctant to challenge the American business establishment that, in their view, calls the shots for America and especially for the powerbrokers in Washington, D.C.